D0508685

LOST LINES:
SCOTLAND
NIGEL WELBOURN

IAN ALLAN *Publishing*

C O N T E N T S

First published 1994
Reprinted 1999, 2001
This impression 2006

ISBN 0 7110 2276 3

All rights reserved. No part of this book may be reproduced or transmitted in any form or by any means, electronic or mechanical, including photocopying, recording or by any information storage and retrieval system, without permission from the Publisher in writing.

© Nigel Welbourn 1994

Published by Ian Allan Publishing

an imprint of Ian Allan Publishing Ltd, Hersham, Surrey KT12 4RG.
Printed by Ian Allan Printing Ltd, Hersham, Surrey KT12 4RG.

Code: 0603/A

ACKNOWLEDGEMENTS
I would like to thank all those who helped me with this book.
In particular, I would like to thank my parents whose patience and understanding when I was younger allowed me to visit so many lines that are now closed.
I would also like to thank all those courteous and helpful railwaymen and women who once worked on the lines mentioned in this book.

Nigel P. Welbourn Dip TP, Dip TS, MRTPI, FRGS.

Cover photos:
Colour-Rail

Right: A morning Ballater to Aberdeen train pauses at Banchory (Dee Street) Halt in August 1965. *A. Muckley*

Introduction

The Scottish Region is the second book in the series 'The Lost Lines'. A cross-section of closed lines have been selected for this volume for their regional interest and for their wider historical, romantic and geographical associations.

In 1923, by amalgamation of smaller companies, the railways of Great Britain were divided into the 'big four' railway companies: the London Midland and Scottish Railway (LMS), the London and North Eastern Railway (LNER), the Great Western Railway (GWR) and the Southern Railway (SR). When these private companies were nationalised on 1 January 1948, the new system — called 'British Railways' — was divided into six regions for management purposes. The new regions included a separate one for Scotland, the others being the Western, London Midland, Southern, Eastern and North Eastern.

This series of books is broadly based on the regions established on nationalisation in 1948. This is because at that time the boundaries selected more closely fitted the earlier constituent companies than those finally arrived at after a number of alterations. In the case of Scotland, the new region was unique in that it covered all the Scottish lines of both former competitors: the LMS and LNER.

Although there had been some closures, at their formation the six regions together covered one of the most comprehensive railway networks in the world. Yet it was clear, even then, that the changing emphases in economic and travel patterns were no longer reflected in the distribution of lines. The problem was compounded in that after heavy World War 2 use, the equipment on many lines was life-expired. Thus it was that the railways at nationalisation

had substantial arrears of both maintenance and investment.

The run-down condition, coupled with the ever increasing 'bite' of road transport meant that financially the railways were no longer in a particularly sound position and British Railways fell ever deeper into debt. As a consequence, in the 1960s notice was served that the complete railway network, which had survived relatively intact up to that time, would be scrutinised as never before. The financial contribution of individual lines was to be examined and it was clear, from the somewhat stringent methods of accountancy, that many would be unlikely to survive on a purely commercial basis. In a surprisingly short time, until the brake was applied, the system was irrevocably reduced in size. By the end of the 1970s over 8,000 miles of line had been closed on the system as a whole, enough to equal the diameter of the world. The closures were on an unprecedented scale.

In the knowledge that change was inevitable, in the 1960s I started to record my travels by train and in the subsequent years I eventually covered, with a few short exceptions, every passenger railway line on each of the six regions. The railway network is much smaller than when I first set out, but my subsequent visits to closed lines show that much survives, displaying a certain grandeur in abandonment. The Scottish Region was also abandoned after four decades of geographical division in favour of other means of organisation, yet much of the past remains in the form of earthworks and an array of structures which have their own fascination; lost to the present, but certainly not forgotten.

3

1 Historical perspective

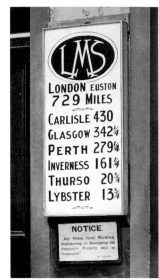

Above left: The crest of the Caledonian Railway Company which swept aside convention by embellishing the Scottish Royal Coat of Arms with its own name. *C. Coles*

Above: The mileage board at a northern outpost in 1931. It's not Thurso, but no prizes for guessing at which station this sign appeared. *H. C. Casserley*

Scotland's first railways developed from 18th century tramways which were built primarily to carry coal from mines to the rapidly growing urban areas of Glasgow and Edinburgh and to the coast. Examples included the Kilmarnock and Troon Railway, which opened in 1812, introducing steam in 1817, and others from the Midlothian mines such as the Edinburgh and Dalkeith Railway built in 1826. Nevertheless, the railway age did not truly arrive in Scotland until the late 1830s and indeed many areas were not served by railways until much later, eg Mallaig in 1901 and Ballachulish in 1903.

Nevertheless, by the mid 1860s there was a growing network of railways in Scotland and almost 150 separate companies had been amalgamated into five leading companies. The North British Railway (NBR) was the largest Scottish railway and fifth largest of all the railway companies at that time. One of its main lines ran over the ill-fated Tay Bridge. Many of its other lines ran from Edinburgh and it was the only company to have its headquarters here, but its freight manager was situated in Glasgow. Its rival, the Caledonian Railway (CR), or 'Caley' as it became known, had an assured charm and grandeur and was the first railway to operate through carriages to London. Then there was the smaller Highland Railway (HR), which in spite of its difficult terrain was a first class main line, running to the most northerly stations in Britain.

The Great North of Scotland Railway (GNSR),

apart from the Campbeltown and Machrihanish, was the smallest of the five Scottish companies, possessing just 334 route miles of line. In its early days it had been renowned for its awkwardness, but it improved to become one of the best loved companies. The line carried mainly passengers and fish and as a consequence had no specifically designed goods engines. Indeed, as wagon labels of the period show, livestock such as sheep and fish were important aspects of Scottish rail freight revenue. Last, but far from least of the pre-grouping railway companies, was the Glasgow and South Western Railway (G&SWR). It served an area that was implicit in its name; this encompassed the Glasgow suburbs and the remote country tracts to the south-west of the city.

The grouping in 1923 of Britain's railways into the 'big four' saw Scotland's railways divided basically between the North British and Great North of Scotland railways, which became part of the London and North Eastern Railway (LNER); and the Caledonian, Glasgow and South Western and Highland railways, which became part of the London

Midland and Scottish Railway (LMS). The LMS was the largest of the four new companies and until 1932 had a larger staff than the British Army. The LMS served Wick, the Kyle of Lochalsh and Oban, whilst the LNER served Mallaig in the west and most of Scotland's north-east coast ports; both companies served Glasgow, Edinburgh, Perth, Dundee and Aberdeen. As the two companies competed to many of the largest Scottish cities, this inhibited rationalisation. Nevertheless, some minor lines were closed in the 1930s and financial pressure on the LMS resulted in some centralising. Lochgorm (Inverness) and St Rollox (Glasgow) locomotive works were downgraded for repairs only and locomotive construction moved to Crewe and Derby, but the real cuts in Scotland were yet to come.

Services suffered a downward drift in World War 2; indeed for a time parts of northern Scotland were

Top: Ex-Great North of Scotland 'D41' 4-4-0 No 62248 on an Elgin to Keith goods in Glen Fiddich in 1952. *W. Anderson*

Above: The former extensive station and modern signalbox at Grantown-on- Spey (West) looking towards Forres in September 1977. Formerly on the main line to London; but trains of the Strathspey Railway will once again run to the town. *A. Muckley*

Right: Lack of investment led to some real antiques being in everyday use in the 1960s such as this NBR hand lamp from Letham Grange. Made by Bulpitt and Sons of Birmingham, it ran on rape oil.

made a protected area, banned to tourists without permit. Equally World War 2 saved branches from closure because there was petrol rationing and road competition was exceedingly restricted. However, the run-down condition of the railways, due largely to their massive war effort, made it necessary that once hostilities ended, either the railway companies were subsidised, or nationalised.

Thus it was that in 1948 the railways were nationalised and grouped into six regions. The whole of Scotland became the single Scottish Region of British Railways. To distinguish the new regions from each other, each was given its own colour scheme which

DUNDEE WEST

V.J. CORASI

reflected, in most cases, distinctive past colouring associated with the region. For the Scottish Region a pale blue colour for the totem signs was chosen. This colour reflected the St Andrew's cross and to some extent the old Caledonian's pale blue livery, which itself was developed as an economy measure when white paint was mixed with Prussian blue to make it go further, but more importantly to produce a very pleasing sky blue effect.

For the first time there was opportunity to consider all the Scottish railways as one entity. The Scottish Region inherited a network of about 3,700 route miles in 1948 that had changed little over the years. There had been very limited new investment. Oil lamps were still the order of the 'night', both to light many rural stations and for general use as hand lamps. There was declining patronage both in freight and passengers and some rationalisation, particularly of old rival lines serving the same destinations, was inevitable. The foundations of many of the lost lines considered in this book were being laid. In 1956 the British Transport Commission, later to become the British Railways Board, closed almost 30 stations on the former Caledonian line between Glasgow and Aberdeen; this was just a beginning!

From 1953 the railways had started to descend ever deeper into debt. In 1961 Dr Richard Beeching became Chairman of the British Railways Board. The two 'Beeching Reports' emerged in 1963 and 1965 and the first, in particular, saw closure of lines as the cure to the ever mounting losses. Between 1962 and 1966 BR closed over 3,000 route miles, of which Scotland

had its fair share. Any remaining duplication and secondary lines were the prime targets, to be eliminated wherever possible. In 1956 it had been stations, but in 1967 the British Railways Board closed sections of the former Caledonian line between Glasgow and Aberdeen itself.

Many Scottish lines passed through sparsely populated areas and the bleak landscape was surpassed only by the bleak finances of some of these routes. However, just as the splendidly attractive West Highland Extension to Mallaig had been subsidised in its construction in 1901, the 1968 Transport Act recognised the need for grant aid and subsidies were again being considered. The social need for lines was becoming increasingly clear; in many areas they represented a lifeline, both for the local economy and in inclement weather. The closure of lines had not transformed the railway's finances and the brake was put on further closures. As a result, some of the more remote Scottish lines that were threatened in the 1960s still remain in use.

British Railways became British Rail and Scottish Region became ScotRail, the shorter name perhaps reflecting the shorter route mileage. However, the traditional pale blue was perpetuated as a stripe in ScotRail's livery. Whilst the concept of the railway region has been replaced by other means of organisation, the identity of Scotland's railways looks set to remain. In the past, most change has resulted in more lost lines being added to the list. Let us hope that future changes will result in more lines being reopened.

2 Geography of the region

The region covered the whole of Scotland although the boundary with England was not quite coterminous with the political border. It included the main cross-border routes from London to Edinburgh and Glasgow. A network of lines covered the Central Lowlands whilst the main route north ran via Perth to Inverness, Wick and Thurso. Another route from Edinburgh served the east coast plains through Dundee and Aberdeen to Inverness, crossing the Firths of Forth and Tay by their celebrated bridges.

There have always been few lines in the remoter parts of Scotland, but the loss of the Waverley route, the Deeside, Fraserburgh and former Stranraer to Dumfries lines have left some large gaps in the map. Yet routes still run west to the Kyle of Lochalsh and Mallaig which serve the Western Isles and to Stranraer, which remains a packet station for Northern Ireland.

Scotland divides into a number of broad physical areas. The rounded Southern Uplands, the Central and Eastern Lowlands and the rugged Highlands all add to the diversity and attractiveness of Scotland's railways. Railway building in such country with its precipitous and diverse landscape and deeply indented coast required some impressive engineering structures such as the Forth and Tay bridges

The region had the greatest number of viaducts, although perhaps surprisingly the fewest tunnels. It is clear that some of the early engineers disliked tunnels; there are just 6 that are over 1,000yd in length. Equally they appear not to have had the same aversion to viaducts and these were occasionally built where they may not have been strictly necessary. There are over 60 that are listed, but many are no longer in railway use.

The railways overcame the demanding Scottish terrain but never misused it; indeed their works are arguably the most distinguished accomplishment of Victorian times in Scotland. Both in war and in inclement winter weather the lines have had deep significance. Most steam became extinct in Scotland in the late 1960s and so did the white-tailed sea eagle. Both have returned. The splendour of much of the countryside, the excitement of the geographical formations and the romantic associations make Scotland's railways, whether open or closed, some of the most attractive in the world. Try a trip and you will soon agree.

Above: Map of Regional Boundaries 1958. *Ian Allan Library*

③ The Waverley route: a long lost line

The long and lovely line from Carlisle to Edinburgh was the last Anglo-Scottish main line to be built and, as with the fate of the Great Central's last main line to London, was one of the first to close. The Waverley route, as it became known, was completed as a through line in July 1862 and soon formed part of the North British Railway which aspired to serve the tweed-making woollen mills in the area and associated towns such as Hawick and Galashiels. After the opening of the Settle and Carlisle line in 1876 the Waverley route carried through traffic including sleeping cars to Edinburgh for the Midland Railway from stations south of Carlisle to London St Pancras. Indeed, through trains from the Border

Right: A Border Television interview team at Hawick station on Saturday 4 January 1969 with the closure protest action group, whose coffin was later loaded on to a London train for delivery to the Ministry of Transport. *J. Arthur McBarr*

Below: Hawick station in quieter times with Ex-NBR 4-4-0 No 62490 *Glen Fintaig* on a passenger train for Carlisle. *N. E. Stead*

Left: Newcastleton station and signalbox, looking south towards Carlisle on 10 September 1968. *A. Muckley*

Below: Although the buildings associated with the station itself have been demolished, Newcastleton station house remains as shown in this photograph taken in March 1993. The line was regarded with affection in the area and many views of the line are to be found in the Liddesdale Hotel at Newcastleton. *Author*

towns used the Midland route to London to the line's very last day. The line later became an arm of the LNER before passing to the Scottish Region of British Railways and was ultimately closed after over 100 years of use.

The route from Carlisle to Edinburgh Waverley went through the smooth rounded hills of the Scottish Borders. Not only was the line itself scenically spectacular, travelling through 'Sir Walter Scott Country' — his first highly successful Waverley novel was written in 1814 — the line became a feature in the unspoilt and open landscape in its own right, with viaducts being as characteristic as the castles and abbeys.

Left: The area could suffer extremes of weather and 'A2' No 60535 *Hornet's Beauty* was blocked in between Whitrope and Riccarton for a fortnight in January 1963. *P. K. Brock*

Below: Great days of the line, 'A2' No 60528 *Tudor Minstrel* passes Whitrope Summit with a northbound special. *A. G. Cattle*

The 98¼-mile line travelling northward from Carlisle crossed the West Coast main line near Kingmore Shed and ascended the Liddel Valley. Although Penton was the first station in the Scottish Region, the first station across the Scottish Border itself was at Newcastleton with its long main street and where nearby the walls of Hermitage Castle stand in the barren countryside.

Once in Scotland the line climbed and curved towards Whitrope Summit to the north of Riccarton Junction before descending steeply through the 1,208yd Whitrope Tunnel, the fourth longest tunnel in Scotland. Continuing northward over Shankend Viaduct it proceeded along the Teviot Valley to Hawick and Melrose. At Melrose there is one of the most attractive Scottish abbeys in the Borders, the 'Kennaquhair' of Scott's story The Monastery. It is therefore fitting that the most graceful of all the stations on the line should be here. The elegant Jacobean style stone buildings are today used as offices, a restaurant and craft shop and are a listed structure of architectural and historic importance.

The Waverley route continued in a north-westerly direction and on to Galashiels, the station which once had the best gardens on the line. It then proceeded with a northward ascent of the Gala Valley and over Falahill Summit north of Heriot. Having thus negotiated one of the most arduous sections of main line,

Above: The bleak south portal of Whitrope Tunnel. The presence of a stream above the tunnel mouth led to instability and substantial retaining walls were provided on either side of the approach cutting. *A. Muckley*

Below: 'A4' No 60031 *Golden Plover* leaving Shankend where it had been diverted on to the wrong line due to engineering works on 18 April 1965. *Ian Allan Library*

Right: Shankend signalbox looking south on 19 February 1983 and in use as a stable; horse below, with hay above. The box is still in existence. *A. Muckley*

Below: Shankend Viaduct on 19 February 1983 looking north. Note the unusual mixed stone and brick construction. *A. Muckley*

trains finally sped on descending grades towards Edinburgh, crossing the River South Esk on a 23-arched viaduct at Newtongrange, before joining the East Coast main line at Portobello.

One of the greatest areas of lost lines and consequently some of the largest gaps in the current railway system was in the Scottish Borders. Much of the Border area of Scotland, particularly between Hawick and Carlisle, is not heavily populated, and in steam days sections of the line required much double-heading, but this major closure in the Scottish Borders was largely the result of rationalisation. The loss of the Waverley route was very much because it was duplicated to some extent by the East and West Coast main lines which both served Edinburgh. In particular, the West Coast line, the old Caledonian Railway's rival route, also ran directly from Carlisle to Edinburgh, but via Carstairs. Although slightly longer, the CR line was less heavily graded and thus competed significantly with the Waverley line, both in speed and operation.

The Waverley main line was the spine of a once extensive network of lost Border lines. The area has been no stranger to passenger closures. The Lauder branch closed as early as September 1932, the line from St Boswells to Reston on the East Coast main

Above: 'B1' No 61290 maintains a full head of steam near Riccarton Junction on the 11.40 am Carlisle to Galashiels goods in May 1961. *Ian Allan Library*

Left: 'J37' No 64608 leaving St Boswells with a pick-up freight for Hawick in July 1961. *J. Baker*

line was first closed by floods in August 1948, the branches to Selkirk and Gretna closed in September 1951 and that from Riccarton Junction to Reedsmouth and on to Hexham in October 1956. The Peebles loop closed in February 1962. The branches from St Boswells to Roxburgh and Kelso, with the two through trains running the 35 miles each weekday to Berwick, together with the branch to Langholm lasted longest, but only until June 1964.

The main line was thus stripped of all its feeder branches and many of the through services were diverted to other routes. Closure finally came, amidst false hopes of reprieves and a chorus of protest, on the first weekend in January 1969 when large crowds turned out to say farewell, the last train of all being the Night Midland sleeper, which was delayed by a demonstration at Newcastleton. A symbolic removal of track took place shortly after, but general lifting took place in 1971/2. Freight remained on the northern section to Hawick for three months longer. There were even plans for a revival using a rake of Gresley coaches, but this came to nothing. Almost a quarter of a century later you can still see many remaining features of the line, although the large stations at Hawick and Galashiels have gone. The gap in the rail map is real and large; this fine main line and the views of this attractive area have been lost to rail travel.

Left: Melrose station was a real gem on the line. This photograph looking west was taken in 1950. *Real Photographs Co*

Centre left: The same view in February 1983 shows the worrying deterioration of this station. *A. Muckley*

Below: In March 1993 a road has replaced the railway, but the station has been restored to much of its former glory. *Author*

Above : The once busy Galashiels station on 9 September 1968 looking north three months before closure. *A. Muckley*

Below: Galashiels station by March 1993 had been completely demolished, but the road overbridge remains. *Author*

Below right: Detail of smashed lamp-post at Melrose station, March 1993. *R. Trill*

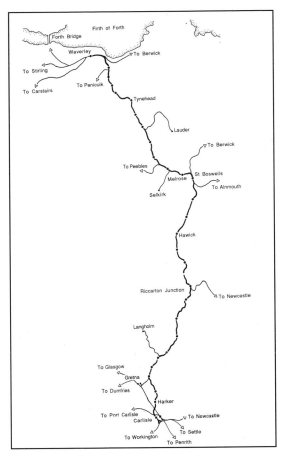

Left: Another view towards Galashiels station taken in March 1993 with the railway signal replaced by a road sign. *Author*

Below left: 'J38' No 65906 passes Eskbank and Dalkeith with a down coal train in July 1960. *J. Baker*

Below: Heriot station and signalbox, looking towards Edinburgh on 9 September 1968. *A. Muckley.*

4 Rush hour at Riccarton junction

Whilst railway lines were constructed mainly to serve existing settlements, in some circumstances railway companies also created their own settlements. Crewe and Swindon are well known, but there were smaller examples. One of the smallest was at Riccarton high in the Border Hills on the NBR's Waverley route. The difficult geography of this Border area provided at Riccarton a natural divergence, allowing a line to run to Reedsmouth, and on to Hexham and Morpeth. However, it was a remote area, away from any settlement or roads. The solution to serve this isolated, but originally important outpost,

Left: General view of Riccarton Junction in 1901. *Author's Collection*

Below: A general view looking east towards Riccarton Junction in 1910. *Author's Collection*

Above right: 'A2' No 60529 approaching Riccarton Junction with a freight bound for Carlisle on a snowy day in December 1961. *W. S. Sellar*

Below right: 'V2' No 60836 passing Riccarton Junction in the background with the 'Granite City' rail tour on 3 September 1966. *P. Robinson*

with its locomotive depot, was to establish in 1862 a new railway town which ultimately contained thirty cottages and was complete with school room, shop and club.

The 'Crewe' of the Borders was thus clearly dependent on the fortunes of the railway; indeed in Riccarton's case there was not even a road connection. Consequently as the Waverley route declined so did Riccarton. The introduction of diesels meant that the Whitrope banking engines were no longer required and once the line to Hexham closed Riccarton's very *raison d'être* was put in doubt. However, it lingered on in a state of growing decline and dereliction, until the closure of the line in 1969. In its last days only two elderly people remained in what was a ghost town of derelict buildings. Today little remains although it is now possible to reach the junction on a forestry road. An extract from my diary

clearly describes the last days of the junction at its peak evening rush hour:

10 AUGUST 1967; We went from Skipton to Carlisle on the Thames Clyde Express. The speed of the train was fantastic, these 'Peaks' really can go. From Carlisle to Riccarton Junction it was found cheaper to pay for a cheap day return to Newcastleton and then pay the guard. When we offered to pay the guard he laughed and told us to keep our money, he would not charge to visit such a place. Riccarton was reached on a beautiful calm evening and once the train had gone not a sound was heard. Everything was derelict and crossing the rusted footbridge it seemed as if no one lived here at all. This was not so, for two people still lived here, an old couple. Everyone else had moved out, dereliction was complete, whole rows of houses lay with smashed windows and deserted. There was however one other person, the signal man, who told us of the former glory of the place when all the row of white painted levers in the signalbox were in use and of trains that ran through to Hexham. On telling the guard we did not pay coming he let us go back free also!

Above: This view taken on 10 August 1967 shows the general desolation of the station. *Author*

Below: 'D49' No 62733 *Northumberland* on the 12.25 pm from Hawick to Carlisle on 1 April 1954. Note that the Riccarton branch of the Hawick Co-operative Society is located on the station. *A. Tyson*

A map of Riccarton Junction shows the difficult and isolated topography of the area as the main line curved its way northward towards Whitrope Tunnel.

There were no roads to the settlement. The extensive earthworks on the Hexham branch at Catscleuch Culvert may explain why viaducts were often the preferred method of construction in such circumstances. Today, the railway tracks and the settlement are no more.

Above: The rather grim Riccarton Junction south signalbox, looking south on 9 September 1968. *A. Muckley*

Right: Even in the remotest of areas there is vandalism. Riccarton Junction south signalbox after closure, in October 1972. *A. Muckley*

Below: The same buildings as opposite in October 1972 with the Co-operative store having long since closed. *A. Muckley*

Left: Inside Riccarton Junction south signalbox on 9 September 1968. Once an important junction for Hexham and Morpeth, the white levers were out of use. *A. Muckley*

Below: Riccarton Junction in 1905 looking north. *Real Photographs Co*

Right: Map of Riccarton Junction in 1923. *Crown Copyright*

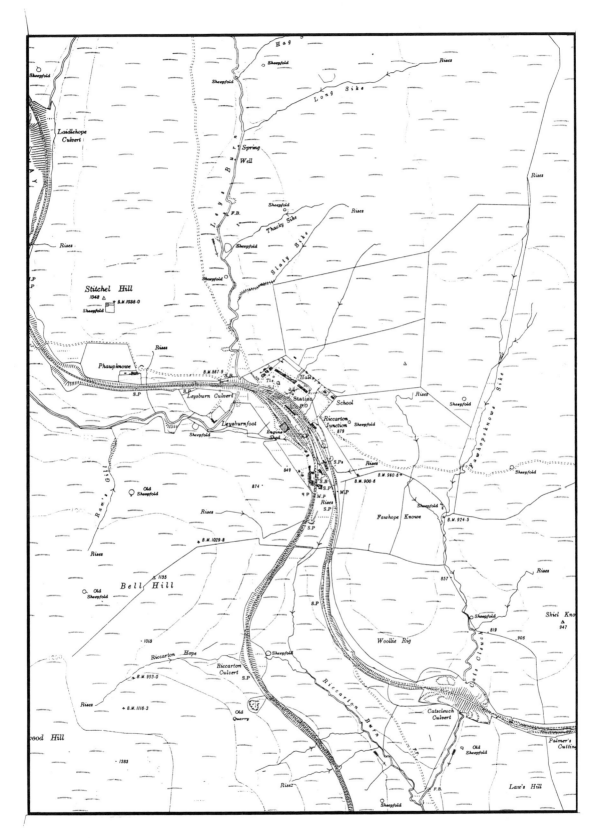

Sheepfold

Laidlehope
Culvert

Levy Burn

Spring
Well

Stitchel Hill
1048 △
☐ B.M.1038·0
Sheepfold

Thacky Sike

Slaty Sike

Hag Sike

Long Sike

Rises

Rises

Rises

Rises

Sheepfold

Rises

Sheepfold

Phaupknowe
△
B.M.867·9

Rises

Leysburn Culvert

Leysburnfoot

Sheepfold

Engine
Shed

Hall

Station

Riccarton
Junction

School

S.Ps

S.P

B.M.900·6

B.M.980·6

Rises

Rises

Sheepfold

Sheepfold

Fawhope Knowe

B.M.924·5

Rams Gill

Old
Sheepfold

Rises

B.M.1029·8

Rises

Bell Hill
△ 1135

Old
Sheepfold

· 1013

Riccarton Hope

Riccarton
Culvert

B.M.993·0

Sheepfold

Woollie Rig

857

Sheepfold

819

Shiel Kno
△
947

·905

B.M.1116·3

Old
Quarry

Riccarton Burn

Catcleuch
Culvert

Old
Sheepfold

Palmer's
Cutting

·1383

Rises

Sheepfold

F.B.

Late's Hill

wood Hill

Above: Riccarton Junction: a view looking north taken in September 1971. *A. Muckley*

Below: Riccarton Junction: a general view of the desolation in September 1971. By 1993 most buildings on the site had been demolished. *A. Muckley*

5 The line that never was

The port of Cairnryan, on Loch Ryan in former Wigtownshire, was built in World War 2 largely as a security measure against the possible bombing of Glasgow's port areas. Initial work on this project was started with some urgency in 1940. Thus it was that a single line military railway was constructed to run northwards some 6 miles between Braid Fell and Loch Ryan to connect this port to a junction on the LMS main line just east of Stranraer.

The route of the line was determined from precise maps made by the 29th Railway Survey Company of the Royal Engineers (RE), which had its base at Longmoor. The construction work was carried out by

contained a network of lines. Military locomotives were used to operate the line and most were small 0-6-0Ts. There were no formal passenger services.

Fortunately the line was never compelled to substitute for any of Glasgow's damaged facilities. Yet it has always been shrouded in mystery because of its military connections. It is generally believed that some 'Mulberry' units, used to form a port in the D-Day landings were made at Old House Point. Some early experimental concrete boats still remain on the coast. The line certainly carried large amounts of ammunition as the surplus boxes were once used for additional seating for Stranraer's football ground on the

Above left: Although the track has long since been removed, the more difficult sections such as this level crossing at Leffnoll remained *in situ* in March1993. *Author*

Above right: A number of barrier gates that protected the line from roads ran on short lengths of rail themselves. This upturned barrier at Leffnoll, where there was formerly a considerable marshalling yard, had yet to be sold for scrap in March 1993. *Author*

RE engineers recruited from the various railway companies of the day. Material for the line was requisitioned from the LMS. It is said that the military authorities were dismayed that the sleepers for the line had been thickly covered in creosote as these would soil the uniformed military personnel constructing the line. There were passing loops and a considerable marshalling yard at Leffnoll Point. At Cairnryan the line ran along the coast and on to a pier that is still in existence, before travelling along the seafront to Cairn Point lighthouse and on to the terminus at Old House Point about half a mile north of Cairnryan.

At Cairn Point two further piers were built. The north pier was constructed of wood, and the south of concrete; both utilised the deep water at this part of Loch Ryan. The line ran on to both piers which were equipped with heavy cranes. The port area itself also

occasion when they had been drawn to play Glasgow Rangers in the Scottish Cup. The coastal line is shown on 1953 Admiralty charts and at that time the piers were clearly a prohibited area.

Although the route was maintained after the war, the 1960s saw its decline. Newspaper articles show

Top: The south pier at Cairn Point was still *in situ* in March 1993. Lines once extended on to the pier which supported a number of heavy-duty cranes. *Author*

Above: Cairn Point Lighthouse, platform and railway buildings associated with the former line. The area was still sealed off from the public in March 1993. *R. Trill*

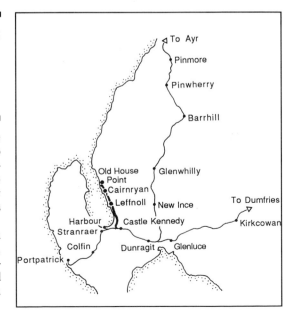

that the line eventually fell into disuse. Although the local authority was anxious for private enterprise to make use of the line, the port and the railway infrastructure were eventually taken over by a ship breaker, who, as it turned out, broke up the railway rather than ships. The line was closed and the cranes and other items were sold for scrap.

In later years another breaker took over and a number of large warships, including the *Ark Royal,* were reduced to scrap. The north pier has been dismantled, but Cairnryan port, just south of the old south pier, is still in use and ferries run to Northern Ireland.

⑥ A lost link to the golf links

Scotland has a powerful golfing tradition, the sport originating here, and Turnberry, with its ruined castle being the reputed birthplace of Robert the Bruce, has developed into one of its most famous golfing resorts. In the early 20th century, travelling from industrial Glasgow to the coast at Turnberry, into this wild area of 'Burns Country', was about as far removed from Glasgow's urbanity as you could get.

Accordingly it was at Turnberry, in May 1906, that the G&SWR opened the 100-bedroom stylish Turnberry Station Hotel. It was publicised in Bradshaw's for its 'electric light, sea water baths, modern sanitation and usually mild and pleasant climate in autumn and winter', a claim that was aided by its location on this part of the west coast of Scotland. The Turnberry Hotel, as it became known, with its Ailsa and Arran golf courses and the former Caledonian Railway's Hotel at Gleneagles are today two of Scotland's leading golfing hotels. Although both hotels on the national-isation of the railways passed to British Transport Hotels, neither is now in railway ownership.

The architect of Turnberry was James Miller. Whilst the hotel has been extended over the years, the tempered Queen Anne charm has been conserved, together with its distinctive contrasting white walls and orange tiled roof. The main hotel building is listed as being of architectural importance.

Also opened in May 1906 was the Maidens and Dunure Light Railway, which was G&SWR-regulated from the outset to encourage interest and connect with its hotel. On Saturdays express services ran from Glasgow St Enoch to Turnberry for golfers. There was also a Euston to Turnberry sleeping car which ran until the line's closure.

The 20-mile single track loop line off the main Glasgow to Stranraer line that served the hotel, ran on the coastal strip between the sea bays of Culzean and Turnberry and the hills of Brown Carrick and Kirk. With the exception of Turnberry, the station buildings were not substantial, but there were extensive earthworks on the line including two curved viaducts and 65 other bridges.

Unlike the hotel, which remains open, the railway line was never particularly successful and had a relatively short life. The 15 miles between Alloway Junction to Maidens and Turnberry closed in December 1930, reopened in July 1932, but closed again in June 1933. The 5 miles from Turnberry south to Girvan closed in March 1942 and the freight service was withdrawn over the entire route in 1955. However, a short northerly section reopened to a holiday camp at New Heads of Ayr in 1947, but finally closed in September 1968.

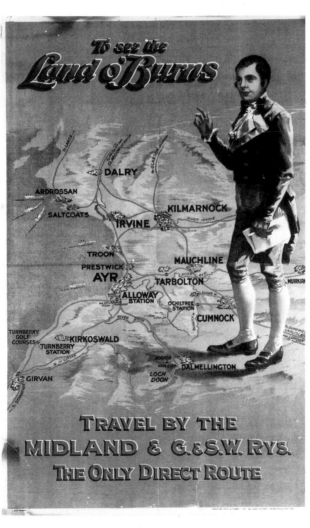

Above: NRM Poster. Many areas of Scotland have great literary connections

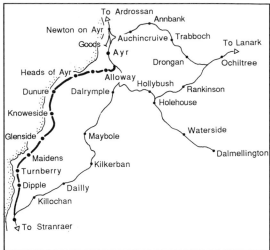

The remains of a station platform and one small building can still be seen in the Turnberry Hotel grounds, whilst some of the lamp posts are of G&SWR design. It is also interesting to note that the front entrance of the Turnberry Hotel is not towards the sea, as you might expect, but faces inland towards the former station to which it was once connected by a covered way.

Above left: Part of the station platform could still be traced at Turnberry in the grounds of the hotel in 1993. *Author*

Below: The 'official' front of the Turnberry Hotel does not, as you would expect, face the sea, but faces inland to the original G&SWR station from which a useful covered link once ran to the hotel. *Author*

7 Leith lines and legacies

The leading seaport for Edinburgh is to the north on the Firth of Forth at Leith. For many years much of its trade was associated with the export of coal and a number of railways were constructed to serve the area. One of the first was constructed by the Edinburgh, Leith and Granton Railway which opened a line from its Canal Street station in Edinburgh to link with the ferries across the Firth of Forth before the Forth Bridge was erected. The line ran at a 1 in 27

gradient down towards Leith via the Scotland Street tunnel, bored through the ridge of Edinburgh and below a number of valuable properties. There was litigation and anxiety as to its stability, but the tunnel opened in May 1847 and carriages freewheeled down, or were hauled up the steep gradient by a cable from a stationary steam engine. Subsequently more lines were built in the Leith area by both the CR and in particular the NBR whose alternative line, opened in

Left: The northern portal of Scotland Street Tunnel taken in June 1993. The tunnel, which passed under the ridge of Edinburgh, was closed almost a century and a quarter ago. *Author*

Below: BRCW Type 2 No D5302 leaving Edinburgh Haymarket on the connection to the old Princes Street line, with the 10.45 am from Waverley for Birmingham on 5 April 1967. It is passing the dismantled overbridge of the connection from Princes Street to Leith. *A. Vickers*

Right: The hanging gardens of Edinburgh! From the Scotland Street goods depot the line headed north towards Leith via this now heavily overgrown tunnel. The photograph was taken in June 1993. *Author*

Below: A Leith North to Princes Street branch train approaching Newhaven on 11 February 1961. Fairburn Tank No 42271 provided a steam service on this day as the regular DMU was in use for an international rugby match at Murrayfield. *W. S. Sellar*

1868, enabled the Scotland Street tunnel and its burdensome gradient to be taken out of use almost a century before the Beeching cuts.

Both the CR, which ran to its own passenger terminal at Leith, and the NBR, which ran to passenger terminals at North, Central and South Leith, also ran a network of freight lines to serve the port. On the passenger side, the NBR's bulky Leith Central terminal station which opened in July 1903 was the most prominent. Indeed, the value of its clock tower was acknowledged by the local authority who paid towards its illumination. Although located centrally in Leith, the line itself succumbed first to trams and then to bus competition for the short journey to

Edinburgh. Leith Central station closed to passengers from April 1952. The administration buildings and shops associated with the terminus remain, together with the clock tower which is still in use, although the vast train shed and much of the solid stone walling have been demolished. The site now provides for water sports and a supermarket.

Services from Leith CR station, which was located within the dock area almost on the Firth of Forth, ran into Edinburgh Princes Street station. Passenger services suffered the same eventual fate as those of the former NBR line, but lasted a further decade until April 1962. Much of this station has also disappeared but the 'Caley' public house opposite the CR station entrance gives a clue to its original location.

Right: The office frontage and clock tower of Leith Central station photographed in June 1993. *Author*

Below: Leith North on 28 April 1962 with the 6.45 pm and last regular passenger train to Edinburgh Princes Street. *W. S. Sellar*

Right: Built to last! The massive train shed at Leith Central has given way to a supermarket and swimming pool. The enormous thickness of walls associated with the station can be seen from this remaining section photographed in June 1993. *Author*

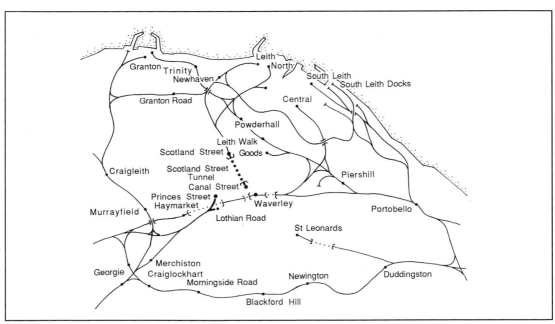

⑧ Edinburgh Princes Street

Edinburgh is known as the 'Athens of the North'. As a consequence of the quality of the townscape, the Edinburgh and Glasgow Railway's original 1842 terminal at Haymarket was located some way from Princes Street and built in a fine classical Georgian manner. The main station building remains, but the original train shed was disassembled in 1982/3 and removed to the Scottish Railway Preservation Society's Bo'ness site for re-erection. In 1846 the line was extended, amidst protests, through the Princes Street Gardens between the Old and New Towns of Edinburgh, to a site near the present Waverley station. The current Waverley station was provided by the NBR between 1892 and 1899 and the low rise buildings, in the open valley in the shadow of the castle, gave added emphasis to the adjacent former North British Hotel. The hotel was opened in 1902 and still dominates Princes Street. Waverley station became part of the LNER and is not significantly changed today, although the station's mosaic heraldic floor was removed by BR.

In the best traditions of competition with the NBR, at the other end of Princes Street, the Caledonian Railway in 1894 eventually decided to build a replacement and much enhanced Princes Street station. This was largely completed by 1899 and the associated hotel was opened in December 1903. Peddie's and Kinnear's immense Station Hotel epitomised the period and added a substantial feature to Princes Street. It had an added quality provided by its construction in blush red Permian sandstone which was brought by rail from quarries in Dumfries. The hotel was connected directly to the station by an impressive

Above: Fairburn Tank No 42273 emerges from the gloom of Princes Street with an evening local to Lanark in August 1964. *I. Krause*

Right: 'Black 5s' with the 11.30 am conveying an interesting collection of through carriages to Manchester and Liverpool leaves Edinburgh Princes Street on 4 July 1964. *W. S. Sellar*

entrance over which the CR's heraldic crest was carved. Indeed, such was the connection with the railway that on one occasion steam from a locomotive was used to provide hot water for the hotel.

The terminal station, which was located at the end of a short spur from Haymarket West Junction, later became the LMS's main station in Edinburgh and in its heyday handled almost 250 trains a day; even in the 1920s it dispatched over 60 suburban trains a day. However, as competition firstly from the tram and then the bus began to bite, the station became less and less used. Rationalisation of the two former competing stations under BR enabled services to be concentrated at the former LNER Waverley station.

Top left: The 1.23 pm Saturdays only train from Glasgow Central arriving at Edinburgh Princes Street on 29 February 1964 behind 'Black 5' No 45467. *D. Smith*

Bottom left: A Carstairs train waits to depart Edinburgh Princes Street on 20 June 1964. *W. S. Sellar*

Top: The Caledonian Hotel frontage, a view that has changed little over the years. *A. McLean*

Right: Princes Street station viewed from the Usher Hall gives an idea of the scale of the station. *A. McLean*

Below right: The deserted interior in March 1965 when the station was a shadow of its former self. Platform 1 is located to the right and platform 7 on the left. *A. McLean*

Indeed, during Princes Street Station's last years it provided a quiet backwater from the bustle of Princes Street itself and the platforms often hosted more parked cars than passengers. Closure of the station came in September 1965. The remaining services were transferred to Waverley station without difficulty and to the benefit of most concerned. After a period of uncertainty, the curving train shed with its deep ridge and furrow roof was demolished. This was unfortunate, but the station entrance gates and main buildings associated with the Caledonian Hotel, were retained.

The station area is now used partly as a car park and partly to provide an extension to the hotel, which remains Edinburgh's only five star hotel. Indeed, the hotel has incorporated the station's lost property office into a bar. The CR's heraldic crested entrance from the station remains within the hotel, together with the station's clock that still maintains accurate time. The stained glass windows that display the coats of arms of towns once served by the CR such as Leith, Alloa and Brechin also remain. The listed former station entrance has been restored and the spur line to the station has been converted into a road.

Far top left: The main entrance to the station with the hotel in the background. *Ian Allan Library*

Top left: Notice of closure at the station's entrance in 1965.
Ian Allan Library

Bottom left: A close up of the station entrance.
Ian Allan Library

Above: The station entrance remains and is a listed structure. In June 1993, when this view was taken, it had recently been refurbished. *Author*

Right: A small section of the station train shed retaining wall still remained in June 1993. *Author*

⑨ Glasgow: a tale of two stations

Glasgow was described by John Betjeman as the finest Victorian city in the world. Situated on the Clyde, it developed as the largest city in Scotland and became the automatic HQ for Scottish Railways both past and present. Indeed, it became the focal point for railways in Scotland in the 19th century, and the Caledonian, North British and Glasgow and South Western Railways all arrived in the city at about the same time. As a consequence, rather as in London,

the separate railway companies each built their own substantial termini in Glasgow.

At the grouping the LMS dominated the city with three main line stations including St Enoch and Buchanan Street, whilst the LNER had one. As a consequence, rationalisation was perhaps inevitable. The loss of Buchanan Street was no great architectural misfortune. A temporary terminus built in 1849 had lasted until its reconstruction and enlargement in

Left: A general view of Buchanan Street station looking towards the buffers on 27 August 1965. *S. Tallis*

Bottom left: The mainly wooden frontage of Buchanan Street station on 27 August 1965. *S. Tallis*

Right: 'A2' Pacific No 60528 *Tudor Minstrel* entering Buchanan Street station with a train from Aberdeen on 2 May 1966. *M. Dunnett*

Below right: A few moments later and *Tudor Minstrel* draws its train towards the buffer stops as Standard Class 5 4-6-0 No 73153 waits to leave with a train to Dunblane. *M. Dunnett*

1933. The new terminus was a functional, low rise and mainly timber-clad building. The station was closed in November 1966 and traffic was transferred to Queen Street. The subsequent bus station built on the site was of equally uninspiring architecture.

St Enoch Station and Hotel were notably more significant and functioned as the Gothic northern companions to St Pancras. The station was of considerable size; its main cylindrical overall roof, over 200ft in width, was only marginally less wide than that of St Pancras whilst the practical Gothic design and ornate ironwork were also genuinely outstanding. It was built by the City of Glasgow Union Railway close to the north bank of the River Clyde and was reached by the first rail bridge across the Clyde. The station was opened in October 1876 by the Prince and Princess of Wales. The St Enoch Hotel was opened in July 1879 and with over 200 bedrooms it was the largest in Scotland at the time. The station was the earliest public building in Scotland to be illuminated by electricity. Four (later two more were added) arc lamps were erected in 1879 working from dynamos driven by steam. Although the carbons lasted only about eight hours, they displaced no fewer than 464 gas lamps which took about 30 minutes to light. The station was vested in the Glasgow and South Western Railway in 1883 and became their main station in the city. Traffic grew and in the early 1900s the station was enlarged by a further 6 platforms covered by a further cylindrical-roofed train shed.

It was at this station in July 1903 that Glasgow's worst railway accident occurred. A train from Ardrossan was in collision with the buffer stops at platform 8, which was not so long as the others and did not extend under the station's overall roof. The inexperienced driver failed to recognise this in time and ran into the buffers at about 10 mph. Unfortunately, the first two carriages telescoped and 16 passengers were killed and 64 injured.

The station had the advantage of serving both north and south Glasgow and three aspect colour light signals were installed by the LMS in 1933. However, a decline in suburban services, resulting from competition by trams and buses, together with a concentration of main line and Ayrshire services to Central station meant that by the 1950s, with the exception of the 'Thames Clyde Express', there were few remaining trains operating from the station. Consequent rationalisation of services to Central station saw this lucrative St Enoch city site as the sacrifice. Other uses were considered, but neglect following closure in June 1966 resulted in the huge twin cylindrical-roofed iron train sheds becoming dangerous and this massive landmark was demolished in 1978, during Architectural Heritage year! The St Enoch Hotel, which occupied the site of an 18th century church and dominated St Enoch Square, was also

Below: Ex-CR 0-4-4T No 55225 on station pilot duties at St Enoch station on 24 July 1961 while in the background 'Black 5' No 45463 waits to depart on an excursion train. *S. Rickard*

Right: LMS Compound 4-4-0 No 40909 with the 9.50 am special Campbeltown boat train to Fairlie Pier. *Ian Allan Library*

Below right: Standard Class 4 2-6-0 No 76093 approaches the station with the 4.11pm from Renfrew (Fulbar Street) on 6 May 1966. This was one of the very few steam-worked passenger trains prior to the closure of the station. *M. Dunnett*

demolished. The site, including the ornate lamp-post standards that adorned St Enoch Square, has been redeveloped as a shopping area.

The name of St Enoch remains as an underground station together with the attractive subway buildings in St Enoch Square. The mosaic floor from the hotel, which incorporates the G&SWR crest, and a large model of the station are to be found in the Glasgow Transport Museum.

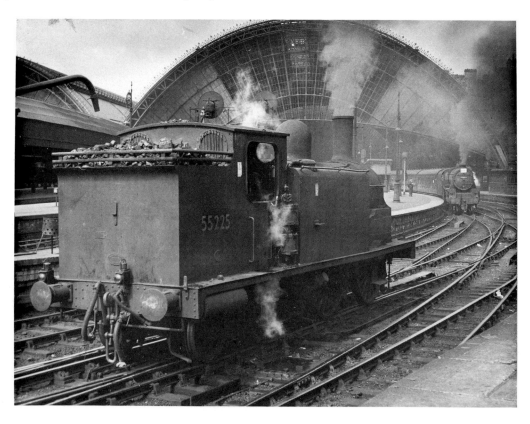

Right: Although the St Enoch Hotel has been demolished, the attractive mosaic floor from its entrance foyer, which incorporated the heraldic crest of the Glasgow and South Western Railway, has been retained and can still be found in the Glasgow Transport Museum. *Author*

Below: An Ayr relief train pulled by Standard Class 4 tank No 80054 departs from the station on 11 April 1966. *D. Cross*

10 Abandoned at Alloa

The port and town of Alloa are situated in the low-lying plain between the Ochil Hills and the head of the Firth of Forth. It was the largest town in the smallest county, Clackmannanshire, which now forms part of the Central Region. The sundial on the house dating from 1695 in Kirkgate has seen many a change, none so great as the rise and fall of railways serving the town. As early as 1767 the Earl of Mar built a 2½-mile tramway to take coal to a bottle works on the Forth. The first line from Dunfermline to Alloa opened in August 1850 and was extended to Stirling by July 1852. By the 1880s Alloa was the centre of a network of lines run primarily by the NBR serving the surrounding coalfield. Lines ran north and west some 5½ miles to Alva and 6¾ miles to Stirling, whilst to the north-east the Devon Valley line ran 17 miles to Kinross. No fewer than two lines ran east some 14 miles to Dunfermline, one near the coast via Culross and one further inland via Oakley. The CR ran a line 8 miles south to Larbert over the Firth of Forth, on the 'other Forth bridge'. This last main link to the town opened in October 1885. The bridge on the line had 20 spans, was 1,600ft long and had a swing section. It was known as the Alloa Bridge and the NBR had running powers over it.

Alloa is not an inconsiderable town, having a population of over 26,000, and even in the 1950s the station boasted almost 40 departures each day. Nevertheless,

Above: The Alloa Bridge signalbox. *Ian Allan Library*

Below: Preserved ex-NBR 4-4-0 No 256 *Glen Douglas* crosses the Alloa Bridge on the former Caledonian branch from Larbert, with the 'Scottish Rambler' rail tour of 30 March 1964. *W. A. C. Smith*

there has been a long history of decline both in freight, which was mainly coal, and in passenger use. The first loss was the passenger service over the coastal route via Culross to Dunfermline way back in July 1930. In November 1954 the Alva line closed and in June 1964 the Devon Valley line closed. This was followed, in January 1968, by the other lines from Alloa West Junction to Larbert, Alloa Junction, over the Alloa Bridge, and finally the 'main line' from both Alloa eastward to Dunfermline and westward to Stirling closed in October 1968.

Left: The Alloa Bridge swing section getting up steam. *Ian Allan Library*

Below: A Park Royal railbus forming the 12.30 Alloa to Larbert service crosses the Alloa Bridge over the River Forth on the last day of service, 27 January 1968. *W. A. C. Smith*

Right: 'J38' 0-6-0 No 65921 passing Alloa Central Junction with a westbound freight on 4 March 1964. The lines diverging to the left ran to Alloa Docks. *S. Rickard*

Below right: The 2.7 pm Stirling to Edinburgh via Dunfermline train arrives at Alloa on 4 March 1964. *S. Rickard*

Left: By June 1993 all the station's buildings had been demolished, but the stone overbridge remained, looking more as if it crossed a river than a railway. Author

Below: After closure to passengers a number of lines remained open for freight and Alloa station is seen here from the cab of a coal train passing through the station on 28 August 1973 hauled by two Class 20s, Nos D8326 and D8327. D. Cross

Right: 'J38' 0-6-0 No 65930 heads a freight on to the Dunfermline line at Alloa East Junction on 4 March 1964. S. Rickard

Below right: The 1.40 pm Dollar to Stirling DMU at Alloa East Junction about to enter the station from the Devon Valley line on 4 March 1964. S. Rickard

Above: 0-4-0 North British shunter No D2710 coming off the Devon Valley line at Alloa with a local freight also on 4 March 1964. *S. Rickard*

Left: A similar view to the previous three shots at Alloa station in June 1993. *Author*

Top right: The site of Alloa East Junction. Note the telegraph pole still survived in June 1993. *Author*

Right: A single track still runs through the Alloa station site and the guiding rail, as it passes under the bridge by the old station platforms, was still in existence in June 1993. *Author*

In 1993 very little remained of Alloa station; the diary therefore illustrates the change in the area from when it was written in 1967:

28 JULY 1967; Travelling over the Forth Bridge the stations at Dunfermline were poor and small. In complete contrast Alloa was a huge old Victorian station with three ticket windows, 5 platforms, ornate iron work and beautiful old lamps.

A map of Alloa shows how this town was once well endowed with railways and tramways. In addition to the main station in the centre of the town there were NBR and CR goods stations to the south. Most industrial areas, which included a shipbuilding yard, were rail-connected. All is now disused, although there remained some freight activity on the lines west of Alloa to Menstrie on the Alva branch and to Stirling until the autumn of 1993. One line was still *in situ* in Alloa station in 1993, the old Edinburgh line, although unused. There are proposals to reopen a section from Alloa to Stirling whose surfeit of platforms would then once again host Alloa trains and, by a slightly circuitous route, Edinburgh would once again be in passenger contact with Alloa.

Far left: Disused track at Alloa leading towards Dunfermline in June 1993. *Author*

Left: The line continues eastward past the Alloa Brewery, but someone has been careful to remove the odd section of track just to make sure that the line cannot be used. This view was taken in June 1993. *Author*

Below left: The abandoned station site with the Alloa Brewery in the background in June 1993. *Author*

Below: Alloa 1901. *Crown Copyright*

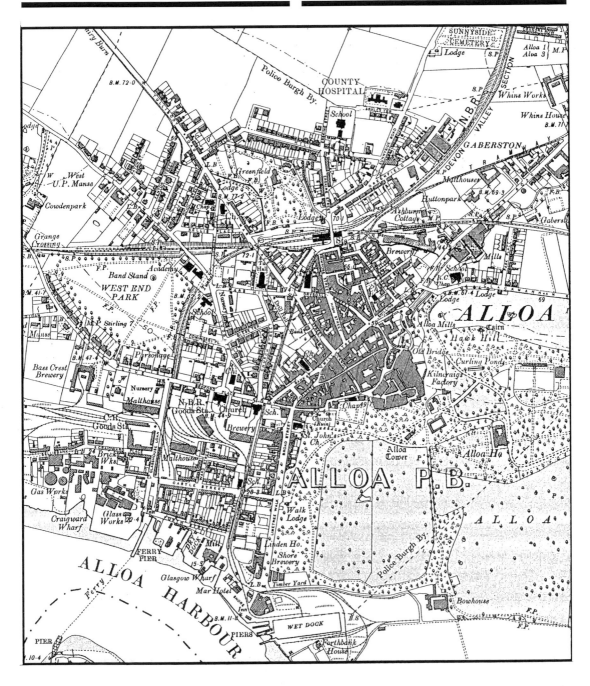

11 Tracks through the Trossachs

From the junction on the Stirling to Perth line at Dunblane, the Caledonian Railway's 40-mile line finally became a through route to Crianlarich in July 1880. It later became the main LMS route to Crianlarich and the Western Isles. The line for the first few miles followed the Teith Valley. It ran through Doune, whose castle was the seat of the Earls of Moray, and on to Callander at the eastern end of the Trossachs, a wild region as shown in the interpretation of its name 'The Bristle Country'.

Left: The listed station house at Doune in June 1993. The station yard has been redeveloped for residential purposes. *Author*

Below: The vandalised Doune signalbox after the line's closure in 1965. *A. Lambert*

Right: 'Black 5' No 45359 at Drumvaich passing place with the 1.18pm Callander to Glasgow Buchanan Street train on 11 September 1965 just before closure. *W. A. C. Smith*

Below: Callander station on 15 April 1963. Camping coaches can be seen on the left as the 12.5 pm Oban to Glasgow and Edinburgh train arrives. The Six Lochs Land Cruise is the second train on the right. *S. Rickard*

From Callander the railway continued northward through the Pass of Leny, along the west side of Loch Lubnaig into more mountainous country and on to the junction at Balquhidder. This is the burial site of Robert Macgregor better known as Rob Roy, but the settlement was some way from the station of that name. This was also the junction for Comric, Crieff and Crieff Junction. The latter was rebuilt in 1919 and renamed Gleneagles to serve the famous hotel of that name.

From Balquhidder, where engines took water for the heavy grades ahead, the main line to the Western Isles continued northward over the 12-arch Glen Ogle Viaduct, crossing a basin in the side of the glen,

Left: Callander West signalbox after the closure of the line. *A. J. Lambert*

Below: The exterior of Callander station which had recently been repainted and was soon to close when this photograph was taken in August 1965. *A. Muckley*

Right: In 1993 the site of Callander station was used as a car park; the road overbridge remains. *Author*

Below right: NB Type 2 Diesels No D6101 and D6127 skirting Loch Lubnaig, between Strathyre and Callander, with the 12.5 pm Oban to Glasgow Buchanan Street train on 12 August 1961. *W. A. C. Smith*

before reaching Killin Junction. This was an extremely beautiful stretch of line and the route itself contained a prize length of perfectly kept track. The remoteness of this area of Scottish lochs is portrayed in Sir Walter Scott's *Lady of the Lake*.

The mountainous terrain meant that this was also a

Above: Balquhidder, looking towards Crianlarich. The passing loop had been taken out when this photograph was taken in August 1965, but the station buildings and canopy over the subway remained. *A. Muckley*

Left: By the time this photograph was taken on 3 September 1966 the station at Balquhidder was disused. The line had not been closed that long, but the station had been ransacked. It was amazing to see the amount of paper country stations generated. Amongst the piles of forms and dockets was a certificate of commendation — a reminder of better days from the past. *Author*

difficult stretch of line to construct, being threatened with avalanches and compelled to climb 941ft to the summit at Glenoglehead. Indeed, for some time during the construction of the route, the terminal of the line was stuck at Glen Ogle, the 'Khyber Pass' of Scotland, and it was a landslip in this general area that saw the premature closure of the line.

At the remote Killin Junction a branch line, opened in March 1886, ran north-eastward 4 miles to Killin and on to the western end of Loch Tay in the shadow

Right: Balquhidder station on 10 September 1983 retains just its subway. *Author*

Below: The 12.12 pm Glasgow to Oban train climbs up Glen Ogle hauled by 'Black 5' No 45173 in May 1955. *W. Anderson*

of Ben Lawers, Perthshire's highest mountain. At Killin Pier ferries once ran along Loch Tay to Kenmore Pier from which Aberfeldy could be reached by coach. The diary records the dilapidated state of Killin station:

SEPTEMBER 4 1965; After a long wait at Crianlarich, to allow the observation car train from Glasgow to pass, the train continued into the mist and on to Killin Junction where the single coach train to Killin itself was waiting. The station at Killin is in very bad condition. When I returned from a visit to the waterfall the man in the booking office said I could not have a ticket until 5.30pm. It was then 3pm. When asked for an explanation as to why, he decided to give me a ticket.

From Killin Junction the main line turned westward to Luib, following Glen Dochart to Crianlarich Lower and on to Oban and the Western Isles.

The 1-mile line from Killin to Loch Tay was closed to passengers in September 1939, and to goods in November 1964, although the shed at Loch Tay remained in use for stabling the locomotives working the Killin branch. The branch from Balquhidder to Comrie was closed in October 1951. The entire main line and Killin branch were due to close in November 1965, but in fact closed at the end of September 1965 owing to a landslip near Glenoglehead, after which trains from Oban were diverted south at Crianlarich on to the former LNER route to Glasgow. The metal bridges and most station buildings were removed, but Glen Ogle Viaduct remains. Killin is now used as a depot and Callander station is a car park. Doune has been redeveloped for housing, although the listed station house remains.

Above left: 'Black 5' No 45016 on the morning pick up freight passing Glen Ogle Viaduct on 9 September 1961. *P. Broun*

Left: 'Black 5' No 45158 *Glasgow Yeomanry* on the 6 pm Glasgow and 5.30pm Edinburgh to Oban train arriving at Luib station on 17 May 1961. This engine was one of the few named members of its class. *M. Mensing*

Above: The Six Lochs Land Cruise on Easter Monday, 30 March 1959 at Crianlarich Lower station. Of note are the brand-new Craven DMU sets and the snow-covered Ben More in the background. *W. Baird*

Below: 'Black 5' No 45124 sporting a snowplough on a northbound freight passes Killin Junction with the Killin branch engine ex-CR No 55222 in the background on 7 March 1952. *W. Anderson*

Above: The Six Lochs Land Cruise (second train) at Killin Junction on 15 April 1963. The DMU leaving in the distance is the Glasgow Six Lochs Cruise which has just come off the Killin branch and reversed for Callander. *S. Rickard*

Below: The Killin branch train is seen here crossing the badly stained castellated stone viaduct over the river at Killin in August 1965. *A. Muckley*

Above: Ex-CR 0-4-4T No 55222 arrives at Killin in September 1958. *D. Penney*

Below: If only Killin had been this busy all the time! The Six Lochs Land Cruise at Killin on 3 April 1961. The DMU had to 'pull up' three times to discharge passengers at the short platform. The train was fully booked. *S. Rickard*

Left: The same view of Killin as previous page, in September 1983. *Author*

Below: Loch Tay was the end of the line and engines working the branch were stabled in the sub shed here. The station itself was closed to passengers and in use as a private dwelling house as this photograph taken on 3 April 1964 shows. *I. Holt*

Right: The abandoned line beyond Killin to Loch Tay on 10 September 1983 with the other Tay railway bridge. *Author*

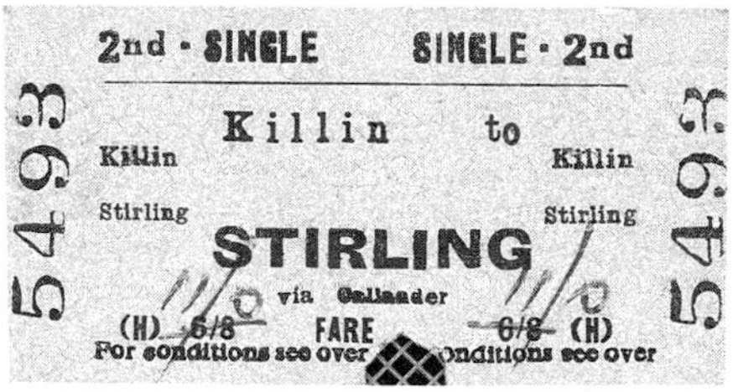

Table 33— *continued*

OBAN, BALLACHULISH, KILLIN, STIRLING, EDINBURGH (Princes Street) and GLASGOW (Buchanan Street)

Week Days only

Miles from Oban	Miles from Ballachulish / Miles from Killin	Station		am	am ❸	am	am	am	am E	am ❸		am ❸	am	am	pm S	am	am S	pm ❸	pm	pm	pm	pm	pm	pm	pm	pm ❸	pm	pm E	pm S	pm S	pm S
		Notes				TC Oban to Glasgow and Edinburgh	Arr Oban 8 48 am	Arr Ballachulish 9 57 am					TC Oban to Glasgow	Arr Ballachulish 11 18 am			RC and TC Oban to Glasgow		TC Oban to Edinburgh except on Saturdays from 2nd July until 3rd September inclusive; RC Oban to Glasgow except on Saturdays until 3rd September inclusive; TC Oban to Glasgow	Saturdays only. TC Oban to Edinburgh. Runs 2nd July until 3rd September inclusive	Arr Oban 1 55 pm			Arr Oban 5 35 pm	Arr Ballachulish 6 24 pm		RC Oban to Glasgow; TC Oban to Glasgow and Edinburgh	SC and TC Oban to London (Euston) arr 7 20 am	SC and TC Oban to London (Euston) arr 7 47 am	Arr Oban 8 30 pm	Arr Ballachulish 10 19 pm
		Oban	dep	..	..	6 5	..	8 25	..	..	..	..	9 18	9 50	..	..	1145	..	12 5	1240	..	..	..	..	4 55	..	5 15	6 0	6 35	..	8 50
—	—	**Ballachulish Z**	dep	..	..	..	7 20	..	..	..	..	..		..	..	10 54	..	..			1227	..	..	4 2	..	..		..	..	7 2	..
—	2	Ballachulish Ferry		..	..	..	7 25	..	..	..	..	..		..	..	10 58	..	..			1231	..	..	4 7	..	..		..	..	7 7	..
—	5	Kentallen		..	..	..	7 30	..	..	..	..	..		..	..	11 5	..	..			1237	..	..	4 12	..	..		..	..	7 12	..
—	8¾	Duror		..	..	..	7 40	..	..	..	..	..		..	..	11 13	..	..			1246	..	..	4 22	..	..		..	..	7 22	..
—	14¼	Appin		..	..	..	7 50	..	..	..	..	..		..	..	11 25	..	..			1 0	..	..	4 32	..	..		..	..	7 32	..
—	17¾	Creagan		..	..	..	7Q57	..	..	..	..	..		..	..	11Q31	..	..			1R 8	..	..	4R42	..	..		..	..	7R42	..
—	20½	Benderloch		..	..	..	8 11	..	..	..	..	..		..	..	11 45	..	..			1 22	..	..	4 56	..	..		..	..	7 56	..
—	27	North Connel		..	..	..	8 17	..	..	..	..	..		..	..	L	..	..			L	..	..	L	..	..		..	..	L	..
6½	27½	**Connel Ferry**	arr	..	..	6 21	8 20	8 49	..	..	..	..	9 34	10 6	..	11 53	12p1	..	1225	1256	1 30	..	..	5 4	5 11	..	5 31	6 16	6 51	8 5	9 6
			dep	..	..	6 22	8 28	8 57	..	..	..	..	9 36	1014	..	..	12 6	..	1227	1 0	1 38	..	..	5 13	5 20	..	5 34	6 17	6 53	8 13	9 15
9½	—	Ach-na-Cloich		..	..	..			..	..	..	..	9 44		..	..	..	..	1235	1 8		..	..			..	5 42	..	..		
13	—	Taynuilt		..	..	6 35			..	..	..	..	9 51		..	..	1219	..	1242	1 15		..	..			..	5Y49	6 30	7 6		
22	—	Loch Awe		..	..	6 54			..	..	..	..	10 9		..	..	..	..	1 —	1 34		..	..			..	6 8	6 49	7 26		
24½	—	Dalmally		..	..	7 0			..	..	..	..	1015		..	..	1242	..	1 7	1 40		..	..			..	6 14	6 55	7 32		
36¾		Tyndrum (Lower)		..	..	7 27			..	..	..	..	1042		..	..	..	..	1 34	2 8		..	..			..	6 42	..	..		
41¾		Crianlarich (Lower)		..	..	7 37			..	..	..	..	1053		..	..	1 20	..	1 44	2 25		..	..			..	6 53	..	..		
48		Luib		..	..	7 47			..	..	..	..	11 3		..	..	..	..	1 54	2 35		..	..			..	7 4	..	..		
—	—	**Killin**	dep	..	7 42	..			..	10 3	..	1055	..		..	..	..	1 42	..	..	..	..	..	..		6 55	..	..	..	..	
51¾	4¼	**Killin Junction**	arr	..	7 55	7 56			..	1017	..	11 8	1112		..	..	..	1 56	2 3	3 0	..	..	..	..		7 8	7 13	..	..	..	
			dep	..	..	7 59	..		..	..	..	..	1114		..	..	..	..	2 5	3 1	..	..	..	..		..	7 15	..	..	..	
59¼	—	Balquhidder		..	..	8 20	..	..	..	..	..	..	1130	..	..	..	1 54	..	2 21	3 17	..	..	..	..	..	..	7 38	8 5	8 46	..	..
60¼	—	Kingshouse Platform		..	..	8b24	..	..	..	..	..	..	..	..	..	..	..	..	2b29	..	..	..	..	..	..	..	..	..	..	..	..
62¼	—	Strathyre		..	..	8 28	..	..	..	..	..	..	1139	..	..	..	2 3	..	2 32	3 26	..	..	..	..	..	..	7 47	8 14	8 55	..	..
70¾	—	**Callander**	arr	..	..	8 44	..	..	..	..	..	..	1155	..	..	..	2 23	..	2 48	3 42	..	..	..	..	..	..	8 3	8 30	9 11	..	..
			dep	7 55	..	8 56	..	..	9 30	..	..	..	12p5	..	1 25	..	2 28	..	2 56	3 47	..	4 0	5 45	..	..	..	8 5	8 31	9 13	..	..
78¼	—	Doune		8 6	..	9 15	..	..	9 41	..	..	..	1216	..	1 43	..	..	..	3 7	3 58	..	4 11	5 56	..	..	..	8 16	..	..	..	..
82	—	Dunblane		8 14	..	9 23	..	..	9 49	..	..	..	1224	..	1 52	..	..	..	3 15	4 6	..	4 19	6 4	..	..	..	8 24	..	..	..	..
87	—	32 **Stirling**	arr	8 26	..	9 34	..	..	9 58	..	..	..	1236	..	2 4	..	2 53	..	3 27	4 17	..	4 30	6 15	..	..	..	8 35	8 55	9 36	..	..
123¼	—	32 **Edinburgh** (Princes St.)	,,	9V50	..	11 3	..	..	11 3	..	..	..	2 23	..	..	..	..	..	4 37	5 23	..	6V33	7 34	..	..	..	9 58	..	..	..	..
117¼	—	32 **Glasgow** (Buchanan St.)	,,	9 13	..	1023	..	..	..	..	..	..	1 39	..	3 15	..	3 41	..	4 22	..	..	5 27	7 11	..	..	..	9 30	..	1027	..	..

b Stops to take up when passengers on platform. Luggage and bicycles not dealt with
E Except Saturdays
L Calls on notice to set down or take up
p pm
Q Calls at **Barcaldine Siding**
R Stops at **Barcaldine Siding** on notice to set down or take up
RC Refreshment Car
S Saturdays only
SC Sleeping Car
TC Through Carriages
V Arr Edinburgh (Waverley)
Y Calls at **Falls of Cruachan** on Saturdays to take up on notice at Taynuilt
Z Ballachulish is the station for Glencoe and Kinlochleven
❸ Third class only

For OTHER TRAINS between Tyndrum and Crianlarich, see Table 34

12 Gleneagles

The Gleneagles Hotel was the concept of Donald Matheson, the CR's Engineer in Chief who in 1910 spent a holiday in Strathearn. He was impressed by the scenery of the area and, with active backing of the CR, work on the hotel began. In order to facilitate construction of such a grand building a goods line was built in 1913. It ran north about one mile from Crieff Junction, later renamed Gleneagles, to the hotel site also of that name. At first the line conveyed the large quantities of stone required to build the hotel, much of which came from a disused railway viaduct. Work ceased during World War 1 and did not resume until 1922. However, in 1923 the CR was absorbed into the LMS and work on the hotel was taken over by the new company with renewed vigour. In June 1924 the hotel was at last opened and the following year the LMS provided the Silver Tassie trophy, the first of many golfing tournaments and events associated with the hotel.

The LMS also retained the railway line which was incorporated discreetly within the hotel grounds, the single line curving around the kitchen garden on an ascending gradient to the rear of the hotel. It remained in frequent use conveying goods, fresh provisions, luggage, laundry, coal for the kitchens and wine from stores at Derby to the hotel.

Right: The substantial Gleneagles signalbox. Not only did the junction serve the Crieff line, it also served the line to the Gleneagles Hotel. *H. Macnamara*

Below: BR Standard Class 4 2-6-4T No 80125 on the branch train at Gleneagles on 30 April 1956. *G. H. Robin*

Far right: NRM Poster. The delights of Gleneagles

Fore!

Gleneagles

The Golf Course the Great
in
Scotland

On the outbreak of World War 2 the hotel was requisitioned by the government for a convalescent hospital, but after this use ended, the railways and their hotels were nationalised and British Transport Hotels took over the hotel and BR the connecting line. At first the line was kept active hauling goods used to return the building to its former use and glory, and the hotel was reopened in April 1947. After reopening, the line was also back in regular use; indeed, it was established that the timetable still accommodated the hotel's requirements as Edinburgh trains had been held an additional three minutes at the station at Gleneagles throughout World War 2 for the hotel's laundry van to be attached!

Although the hotel merited its own luggage label, the line did not have a regular daytime passenger service; guests arriving by rail were, and still are today, mainly collected by road from the station for the short beech-lined drive to the hotel. Nevertheless, sleeping coaches were shunted up the branch and there were some other extraordinary passenger services. For example, the Maharajah of Bhopal arrived in a special train and the World War 2 railway car of Winston Churchill, which was turned into a miniature Indian Palace, was manoeuvred right up the line to the hotel's rear entrance.

With the growing use of motor transport, decline in the use of the line set in and it was closed by 1966 as one of the Beeching economies. The line of the track can still be traced through the hotel grounds, and towards the station at Gleneagles. The LMS plans for the hotel and its railway remain on view in the hotel; in 1994 one member of staff remained a member of a railway union, and of course Gleneagles station is still open.

Above: The main entrance to the Gleneagles Hotel photographed in the 1930s. Only the design of cars has changed. *British Railways*

Left: Class 40 No 265 on the 07.20 Aberdeen to Glasgow train passing Gleneagles on 3 May 1971 by this time the extensive trackwork associated with the junction had all been removed. *J. H. Cooper-Smith*

Below: The Gleneagles Hotel and golf course photographed on 19 July 1930. *British Railways*

13 Bridge to Ballachulish

The 28-mile line from Connel Ferry to Ballachulish was opened by the Caledonian Railway in August 1903. Originally it was intended to continue to Fort William and thence up the Great Glen directly to Inverness, but crossing the deeply indented Loch Leven, which flows into Loch Linnhe at great speed, made this aspiration expensive and it was never achieved. The line later became a backwater of the LMS and the Scottish Region.

The line ran northward from Connel Ferry Junction, over the Connel Ferry Bridge. This unique and imposing cantilever bridge is the second largest of its type in Britain. It was built by the CR with an eye to being shared by both trains and road traffic as a considerable detour was necessary if the bridge was not used. At first the CR asserted that motor vehicles should be carried across the structure on a rail vehicle, but later a single carriageway road was

Right: The scale of Connel Ferry Bridge can be judged from this photograph with the 10.48 am Ballachulish to Connel Ferry train being hauled by ex- CR 0-4-4T No 55238 on 21 May 1960.
M. Mensing

Below: Connel Ferry Bridge with a Connel Ferry to Ballachulish train hauled by ex-CR 0-4-4T No 55208 on 14 May 1958. *I. S. Pearsall*

squeezed in beside the railway line. This was closed when trains crossed, whilst equally trains waited for the road to be closed. Tolls for crossing the bridge were considerable and came in for fierce criticism when they were retained after the railways were nationalised in 1948. At that time the charge for a private motor car varied from four to six shillings (20–30p), a hearse was charged seven shillings and six pence (37½p), sheep and pigs were charged sixpence each (2½p) and cows nine pence (4p); bulls

Left: The gatehouse at the southern end of Connel Ferry Bridge photographed on 15 November 1953. The view shows that in addition to being closed when a train crossed over the bridge, the road itself operated only on a one way basis. *Ian Allan Library*

Below: The bridge was shared by a road but, as can be seen from this photograph with an ex-CR 0-4-4T No 55263 crossing the bridge in August 1959, it would have been a tight squeeze for a lorry passing in the opposite direction. *P. Ransome-Wallis*

Right: Ex-CR 0-4-4T No 55263 approaches Connel Ferry. The ex-Caledonian Railway signals on this line were particularly attractive, such as this old two way lower quadrant post. *M. Ware*

Below right: North Connel station as seen from the train in August 1965 during the last summer of operation on this line. *A. Muckley*

however were charged one shilling (5p). The bridge carried the railway over Loch Etive where a narrow gap creates a waterfall at ebb and flood tides which have been made well known by the mythical poet Ossian as the Falls of Lora.

The line continued northward by Ardmucknish Bay, skirting the coast in sight of the twin peaks of Benderloch. It then passed over Creagan Viaduct which was constructed of two steel trusses with castellated stone arches at each end. The line con-tinued along the coast of Loch Linnhe before turning eastward along Loch Leven to reach Ballachulish.

Timetables have always made it clear that Ballachulish was also the station for Glencoe, with its dark events of 1692, and that there was a connecting ferry service to Kinlochleven, perhaps in small compensation for the fact that the original intention was for Inverness to head the timetable.

The line suffered temporary closure due to floods in 1953. In its final days the track was overgrown and

Above left: Benderloch station with its platform canopy looking rather the worse for wear in August 1965. A. Muckley

Below left: The island platform at Creagan station looking towards Connel Ferry in August 1965. A. Muckley

Above: D5349 with the 12.35 pm Connel Ferry to Ballachulish train crossing Loch Creran, a sea loch branching off Loch Linnhe. Diesel locomotives took over workings during the summer of 1962. C. Bowman

Right: A freight train awaits 'the road' at Appin station on 6 July 1956. Dr E. M. Patterson

Left: Duror station, looking towards Ballachulish, and in a rather better condition than Benderloch station although also photographed in August 1965. *A. Muckley*

Below: 0-4-4T No 55263, a frequently photographed engine at Ballachulish station, the end of the line. *Ian Allan Library*

the lattice post semaphores rusted through by the sea air. The diary records a trip in its penultimate year:

30 AUGUST 1965; Went on line from Oban to Ballachulish. The carriage was in a disgusting state. Pictures had been turned back to front and drawn on, paint had been put on the seats which had been slashed. Signal posts were brown with rust and the track was overgrown with a grass-like plant. On first sight it looked as if the line was already closed.

The branch was thus in a run-down condition when it closed to freight in June 1965 and to passengers in March 1966. Track lifting began shortly after, but the fine bridges at Connel, which no longer charges tolls, and Creagan remain.

Right: BRCW Type 2 No D5364 prepares to leave Ballachulish with the 4.10 pm to Oban on 3 April 1964. *I. Holt*

Below: Ballachulish, the end of the line, in November 1969. *A. Muckley*

14 A Fife fatality

The Fife peninsula, between the Forth and Tay estuaries, was noted prior to World War 2 for coal exports, particularly to the Baltic countries. The district comprised a network of lines, several of which were mineral only lines, that linked coalmines to ports developed round the Fife coast by the NBR. A characteristic example was the 14½-mile freight only line from Leven on the coast to Lochty. The line curved north-eastward soon after leaving Leven to run north of Largo Law to its terminus at Lochty. The route was opened in August 1898 by the NBR.

The line served the agricultural hinterland of Fife, but as traffic declined, the branch was worked in its final years on the one engine in steam principle. This is an interesting example of a line that closed, reopened in part and then closed again. The route,

Left: 'J35' No 64488 shunts at Largoward goods on the branch from Leven to Lochty. *Hugh Davies*

Below: Super power with an 'A4' Pacific No 60009 hauling a single observation coach on the Lochty Railway in 1968. *D. M. C. Hepburne Scott*

which never had a regular passenger service, first closed in August 1964 and a number of short sections were converted to farm tracks. However, a local farmer purchased a 1½-mile section and formed the Lochty Private Railway. On this short line was run the ex-LNER 'A4' Pacific No 60009 *Union of South Africa* (later changed to *Osprey*) and the LNER Coronation beaver-tailed observation car, together with other assorted rolling stock.

Passenger services started in 1968, but in 1973 No 60009 went on to return to main line specials, although a Bagnell Austerity 0-6-0T from the Wemyss Private Railway and a Peckett 0-4-0T of 1915 vintage from British Aluminium at Burntisland continued to run on the line. However, these never held the attraction of the 'A4' and, with the costs of meeting new health and safety regulations and a somewhat isolated location, the line's last full season was in 1991. Much stock has since been dispersed, including items to the Caledonian Railway Society at Brechin, although the observation car has gone to the Great Central Railway at Loughborough.

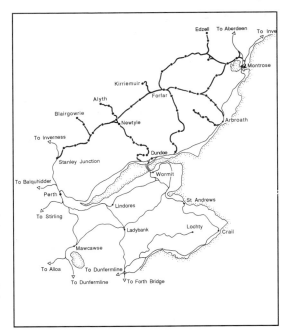

Right: One of the ex-LNER distinctive beaver-tailed observation cars which had such a varied career starting on trains to mark the coronation of King George VI. Here shown on the Lochty Railway. *M. Fox*

Below: The Lochty Railway was to close and the stock was dispersed; this view is of the line at Lochty in September 1983. *Author*

15 Dundee directory

Bouch (Thomas) was an engineer noted for his economical schemes. The first Tay Bridge was conceived by Bouch, who for his efforts became Sir Thomas Bouch and a Freeman of Dundee. The bridge was built mainly in wrought iron fabricated at Wormit, which is located at the southern end of the bridge. The centre spans at 79ft above the Tay, for navigational clearance reasons, were known as the 'high girders'.

McBeth (David) was a guard on the night down mail to Dundee on Sunday 28 December 1879. The

Left: The original single line Tay Bridge under construction showing a contractor's locomotive *circa* 1877/8. *British Railways*

Below: The old Tay Bridge looking decidedly spindly *circa* 1877/8. *British Railways*

Right: A rather morbid postcard available after the accident. *Ian Allan Library*

Below: The Tay Bridge from the north after the accident in 1879. *British Railways*

OLD TAY BRIDGE DISASTER, 1879: FALLEN GIRDERS

topography of the Firth of Tay compounds the effects of high winds and a storm of hurricane force on that evening resulted in failure of 13 central girders of the bridge, casting the train and its 75 passengers and crew into the freezing waters below. All lives were lost. The accident was said by some to be divine retribution for running trains on the sabbath, but it forced the Board of Trade to issue new regulations relating to railway bridges. In recent years the blame has shifted more to question defective materials, or even a buckled rail, rather than just bad design. Only the locomotive, NBR No 224, survived the disaster, being salvaged from the Tay and repaired at Cowlairs to run until 1919 in Scotland.

McGonagall (William) was a poet who wrote some memorably bad lines. However, Scotland's first great railway tragedy resulted in Scotland's best known railway poem *The Tay Bridge Disaster,* some verses of which are set out on the following page:

Left: The new Tay Bridge in 1946 showing the footings of the original lost bridge. *H. C. Casserley*

Centre left: Looking beneath the Tay Bridge at the stumps of the lost bridge. *H. C. Casserley*

Below left: A footplate view from 'Black 5' No 45487 on a northbound Edinburgh to Aberdeen goods crossing the 'high girders' of the Tay Bridge on 21 February 1953. *E. Patterson*

Right: 'J37' 0-6-0 No 64602 at Dundee West about to move stock to Dundee Tay Bridge station where it was to form a special excursion round the East Fife line on 1 May 1965. *Ian Allan Library*

Below right: Standard Class 5 No 73148 pulling out of Dundee West station with a Glasgow train in March 1958. *W. Anderson*

Beautiful Railway Bridge of the Silv'ry Tay!
Alas! I am very sorry to say
That ninety lives have been taken away,
On the last Sabbath day of 1879
Which will be remember'd for a very long time.

So the train mov'd slowly along the Bridge of Tay,
Until it was about midway,
Then the central girders with a crash gave way,
And down went the train and passengers into the Tay!

The Storm Fiend did loudly bray,
Because ninety lives had been taken away,
On the last Sabbath day of 1879,
Which will be remember'd for a very long time.

I must now conclude my lay
By telling the world fearlessly without the least dismay,
That your central girders would not have given way,
At least many sensible men do say,
Had they been supported on each side with butresses,

At least many sensible men confess,
For the stronger we our houses do build,
The less chance we have of being killed.

The lesson was learnt; the present Tay Bridge was built more substantially and as a double track bridge. Since its opening in 1887 it has endured such storms. It is the longest in Britain and among one of the longest in the world at 2miles 50yd. It was constructed on completely new foundations by the NBR. Although

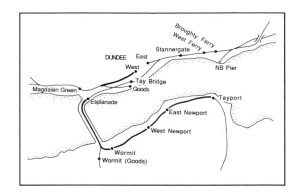

a number of the old girders were reused, the high girders were replaced. The original bridge footings can still be seen just above high water to act as cutwaters downstream of the present bridge, a grim reminder of the lost line of the first Tay Bridge.

Barr (Thomas) was an engineer in chief for the Caledonian Railway. He was responsible for the design of a number of stations, but one of his most outstanding was Dundee West. The station was built in 1889 and was devised in a Scottish baronial style of architecture as far as this could be applied to stations. With its dominating red sandstone and turreted façade, attractive train shed and impressive clock spire, it was particularly fine and a great credit to Dundee.

Dr Beeching (Richard) was Chairman of BR in the 1960s. There are those who consider that descriptions such as memorably bad, or hurricane force may apply

to his term of office. He had no direct connection with Dundee, but he certainly had an effect on the railways in this part of Scotland, closing lines and stations in the area. For his efforts he became Lord Beeching. The first station at the very northern end of the Tay Bridge, Dundee Esplanade, was closed long before Beeching's time — as far back as October 1939 — and the short line from Camperdown East Junction to Dundee East closed in January 1959. Yet it was the closure of the equally short spur from Buckingham Junction to Dundee West from May 1965 that led to one of the most attractive city stations in the whole of Scotland being demolished. Finally, the construction of the Tay Road Bridge resulted in the replacement of the Tayport to Dundee, Wormit Junction, trains between Newport-on-Tay and Tayport by buses in May 1966 in order to facilitate construction of the new bridge. However, the connecting rail service from Newport succumbed in September of the following year.

Dr J McIntosh Patrick is the artist whose studio overlooks the Tay Bridge. His pictures of the Tay Bridge are in addition to his sketches for railway carriage panels and his designs for posters for London Transport and other main line companies. The subjects usually, but not always, have a Scottish theme and include a number of locations on lines that are now closed.

ST. ANDREWS

GUIDE FREE FROM TOWN CLERK, ST. ANDREWS, FIFE

Train services and fares from BRITISH RAILWAYS stations, offices and agencies

Left: Tayport station on 2 May 1966 before trains were replaced by a bus service to Newport-on-Tay later that month to facilitate construction of the Tay road bridge. *W. S. Sellar*

Top right: NRM Poster. An example of McIntosh Patrick's work on a lost line

Right: Tayport station on 4 July 1966 barely six weeks after its closure. The track heading towards Newport-on-Tay and the new Tay Road Bridge had already been removed and the replacement bus service is evident. *J. Boyes*

16 Strathmore: service suspended

Dundee is backed by the Sidlaw Hills and to the north of these is the valley of Strathmore, which means the Great Vale. The CR named this area 'Shakespeare Country', because the general landscape was not dissimilar to Warwickshire, and the ancient castle of Dunsinane could be observed in the far distance. In fact other names may have been more appropriate as Glamis and its castle, a royal birthplace and

Left: 'Black 5' No 44997 shunts in the yard at Coupar Angus after arriving with the freight from Perth on 31 May 1966. *C. Bowman*

Below: Returning from Forfar with the daily branch freight Class 26 No 26027 passes the derelict station at Coupar Angus as it heads for Perth on 2 September 1981. *B. J. Beer*

Above: The remains of Coupar Angus on 10 June 1993. A decade of disuse has seen the vegetation overtake the site. *Author*

Left: Coupar Angus signalbox in September 1983 after track removal and complete closure. *Author*

famed for its possible secret room, were located much closer to the railway, whilst at Guthrie the line was forced to disguise its bridge over the castle's very entrance as an antiquated arched gateway.

It was through this area that the main Caledonian and later LMS route to Aberdeen ran for 46 miles from Stanley Junction via Coupar Angus, Forfar and Bridge of Dun to Kinnaber Junction near Montrose. The line developed from a number of early independent railways, but operated as a through route from July 1856. Although not originally built as a main line and containing a mass of junctions, the route provided one of the first frequent British 60 mph runs between Forfar and Perth.

The main line was the spine of a network of branch lines which provide a catalogue of suspended passenger services. Travelling east from Stanley Junction the first connection could be made at Coupar Angus, where trains ran to Blairgowrie on the edge of the Highlands. This service was suspended in January 1955 and today only a very small part of the sturdy red sandstone terminus station at Blairgowrie remains. At Alyth Junction a branch ran north to Alyth, but was one of the first to lose its passenger services in July 1951, whilst a second branch ran south to Dundee via Newtyle. Although this line was later rerouted, the original 1836 station at Newtyle, which was served by a rope incline, had the earliest overall through station roof in Scotland. Passenger trains ended in June 1955, but Newtyle station remains in its isolated position today.

Above: Coupar Angus signalbox has remained largely intact over the last ten year period, as this photograph taken in June 1993 shows. *Author*

Below: Coupar Angus was the junction for Blairgowrie. The ex-Caledonian train shed at Blairgowrie is shown here in June 1975. *Author*

Below: The fine red sandstone terminus at Blairgowrie was almost unchanged in June 1975 even though it had closed for passengers twenty years earlier. *Author*

Right: By September 1983 Blairgowrie station had been obliterated within an industrial estate. *Author*

Centre right: Although all the track had been removed, the blue enamel sign for Alyth Junction could still be spotted amongst the dereliction in September 1983. *Author*

Below: South of Alyth Junction lies Newtyle station. The overall roof is the earliest in Scotland and the station buildings remain today almost as originally built. *Locomotive Publishing Co*

Above: Kirriemuir was the end of a branch from Kirriemuir Junction which closed to passengers in 1952 and freight in 1965. This photograph shows freight being shunted by steam at the terminal together with a horse and cart; a whole way of transport about to be obliterated. *Hugh Davies*

Left: One of the most famous locations on this line was Glamis Castle. Although the station of that name was some distance from the castle, its tourist potential was clearly recognised by both the LMS and LNER as this poster in the Glasgow Transport Museum shows. *Author*

Above right: The 8.15 am Glasgow Buchanan Street to Aberdeen train leaving Forfar behind 'Black 5' No 44786 on 4 February 1961. *W. Sellar*

Right: Ex-CR 0-6-0 No 57441, fitted with an NB chimney, shunting on the branch to the original 1838 passenger terminus at Forfar on 25 February 1961. *W. A. C. Smith*

From Forfar passenger trains connected with Kirriemuir Junction and Kirriemuir until August 1952. Two secondary routes also ran from Forfar. Up to January 1955 a connection could be made to Dundee while a second line diverged in a loop to run in a generally north-easterly direction, to rejoin the main line at Bridge of Dun. A triangular spur was provided off this loop to enable trains to call at the terminal at Brechin, and a branch ran north to Edzell which

Above left: 'Black 5' No 44999
passing Forfar Junction with an up
fish train on 25 July 1955.
K. L. Cook

Left: BR Standard Class 5 No 73008
awaits at Careston on 19 May 1964
prior to return to Forfar with the
Tuesdays and Thursdays only
freight, on this section of the former
Brechin branch. *J. Spencer Gilks*

Above: 'V2' 2-6-2 No 60919
departs from Bridge of Dun with the
07.15 Perth to Aberdeen local on
13 August 1966. *M. Burns*

Right: 'J37' 0-6-0 No 64577 sets
out from Bridge of Dun along the
branch line to Brechin on
23 September 1965. *M. Dunnett*

closed, apart from a short period in 1938, to passengers as far back as April 1931. The station at Brechin was built in 1847 and extended in 1894-5 for the Caledonian Railway. Brechin and this loop section closed to passenger traffic in August 1952, but the attractive terminal station at Brechin has been leased to the Caledonian Railway Society who have reopened

a section of line and now run trains along the South Esk to Bridge of Dun.

From Forfar the main line proceeded to Guthrie, where up to December 1955 passenger trains ran through to Arbroath. It then ran via Bridge of Dun, where the loop from Forfar rejoined the line, before continuing to Dubton Junction, where until August

Above: D5126 on the 17.15 Aberdeen to Glasgow relief train passing Bridge of Dun with its neat flower-beds on 8 July 1966. *J. Boyes*

Below: Class 26 No 26023 threads the remaining track at Bridge of Dun with a daily goods from Montrose to Brechin on 17 November 1980. All traffic to and from Brechin ceased at the beginning of May 1981 until the Caledonian Railway (Brechin) took over the line. *Ian Allan Library*

Right: 'J37' 0-6-0 No 64602 climbs away from Bridge of Dun with the daily freight on the Brechin branch on 18 May 1966. *W. A. C. Smith*

Below: 'J37' 0-6-0 No 64611 on the daily freight from Montrose to Brechin climbing the 1 in 90 gradient in the vicinity of Arrat's Mill on 23 March 1967. *C. E. Weston*

1952 passenger trains ran to Montrose. Having passed over a succession of no fewer than seven junctions since Stanley Junction the main line finally reached Kinnaber Junction.

The main line, having been stripped of all its connecting passenger services, saw its remaining passenger traffic diverted via Dundee and Arbroath, and it closed in September 1967. Freight lasted longer; on some sections west of Forfar and east of Brechin until the early 1980s, but apart from the Caledonian Railway Society's ambitions there is today little activity. The wooden station buildings that still

Above left: 'J37' 0-6-0 No 64577 shunts in the overgrown yard at Edzell on 19 May 1964 having come from Brechin with the 'when required' freight service. This service has now long since been withdrawn. *J. Spencer Gilles*

Left: 'J37' 0-6-0 No 64620 with the 13.20 Montrose to Brechin pick-up goods in Brechin yard on 7 July 1966. *J. Boyes*

Above: 'J37' 0-6-0 No 64620 on the 13.20 Montrose to Brechin pick-up approaching Brechin on 7 July 1966. The Brechin locomotive shed is on the centre right whilst the former line to Edzell runs off into the trees on the left. *J. Boyes*

Right: A taste of the future with EE Type 1 on a special train at Brechin on 22 April 1962. *R. B. Parr*

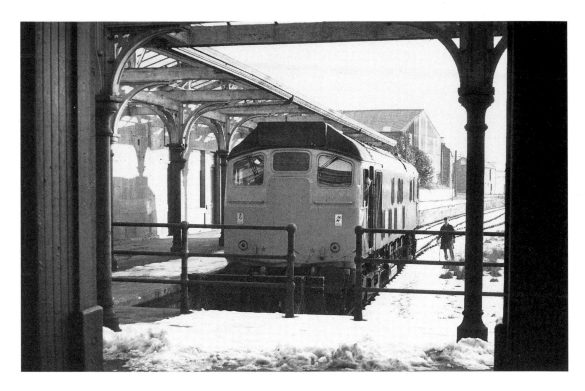

existed at Coupar Angus in 1983 had gone a decade later and at Forfar the station site has been used for housing.

As an aside, the coastal line on to which the traffic was diverted also contained an interesting line up Elliot Water to a terminus north-east of Carmyllie. This 4½-mile line was constructed at the expense of Lord Dalhousie to transport rock from the quarries near Carmyllie to Elliot Junction on the main line. The line opened in 1854, but a passenger service ran only between February 1900 and December 1929. The line closed in 1960, but was distinctive for incorporating a 1 in 35½ adhesion gradient, the most precipitous in Scotland worked by passenger trains.

Above: Brechin on 5 February 1979 with Class 25 No 25009 running round after arrival on a freight from Dundee and Montrose. *R. E. Ruffell*

Left: 'B1' 4-6-0 No 61277 at Elliot Junction with the Carmyllie branch to the right. *T. G. Hepburn*

Right: Map of Brechin in 1927. *Crown Copyright*

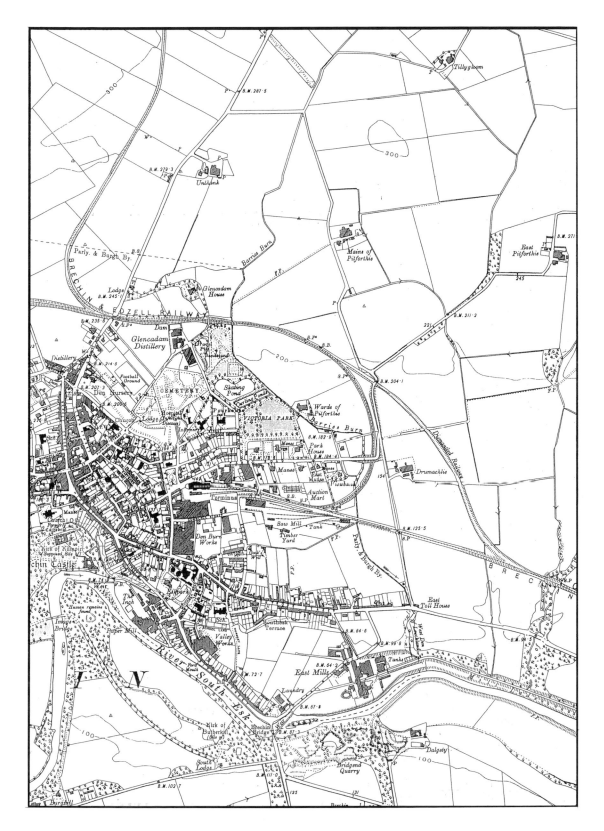

Right: Ivatt 2-6-0 No 46463 in woodland north of Elliot Junction on the line to Carmyllie on 7 May 1959. *D. Capper*

Below: The Carmyllie branch approach to Elliot Junction on 27 May 1960. *T. G. Hepburn*

17 Decline on Deeside

The Great North of Scotland Railway's 43-mile Deeside branch, which opened in stages to Banchory in 1853, Aboyne in 1859 and in October 1866 to Ballater was used by royalty on their way to Balmoral Castle. Before the line passed to the GNSR, the Strathspey, Strathdon and Deeside Junction Railway had ambitions to extend the line from Ballater through Tomintoul and Nethy Bridge to Inverness over the Grampian Mountains, but the proposed mountainous route was never built.

Although Queen Victoria made use of the line, another proposal to extend the branch to Braemar was objected to as it would have taken the railway too close to her estate at Balmoral. Indeed, such was the supposed threat of railway development that when in 1868 a local landowner started to extend the line

Above: 'K2' No 61782 on the 10.15 am Aberdeen to Ballater train passing Ruthrieston in July 1953. Note that the lifting of the second track is in progress. *Ian Allan Library*

Right: Battery railcar units were used on the line as an experiment in the late 1950s. This photograph shows the battery cradle section which weighed eight tons in total under one of the coaches. *British Railways*

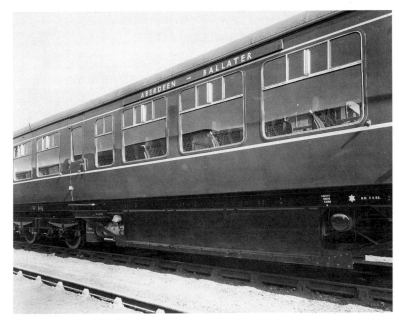

towards Glen Gairn to convey timber from his plantation, even after rails had been laid, Queen Victoria bought the forest and the line was removed. A road that subsequently used a section of this route is known as 'the Track of the Old Line' and can still be traced on maps.

Thus it was that although Ballater station was optimistically not built as a terminus, it remained the end of the line. As a compromise, lorry and bus connections were initiated to Braemar as early as 1904. The single story wooden terminal at Ballater constantly hosted royal trains which worked the branch on many occasions when royalty used Balmoral. Special trains also ran until 1938 conveying dispatches to Aberdeen to connect with the London trains. In days before the

Left: A poster extolling the virtues of Ballater in the Glasgow Railway Museum. *Author*

Below: The 6.45 pm leaves Banchory for Ballater on 31 July 1964. *P. Wells*

Above: Less than a decade later the remains of Banchory station, looking towards Aberdeen in February 1972. *A. Muckley*

Right: A busy scene at Torphins station at the turn of the century. *Ian Allan Library*

improvement of telecommunications, such was the isolation of Balmoral that these trains operated even on Sundays when the remainder of the branch was closed.

The branch ran westward from Ferryhill Junction just south of Aberdeen's Joint Station and up the Dee Valley from the 'granite city' into the Grampian Mountains, which sweep up to heights of 3,500ft. The greater distances between stations as the line ran inland, past Crathes and Aboyne stations and their castles, were clear witness of the reducing population as the line proceeded, by woodland and moorland, up the north side of the Dee Valley towards its enforced terminus at Ballater.

The line passed to the LNER and later to BR who in 1958, for a period of about three years, ran two-car

Left: Torphins station and signalbox looking towards Aberdeen in May 1970. *A. Muckley*

Below: The spires and towers of Aboyne station exterior in May 1970. *A. Muckley*

battery-powered electric railcars on the branch. Stationary charging plants were installed at Ballater and Aberdeen. The units were well received, particularly for their silent running, but they were limited to 50mph because of track constraints on the branch. However, in spite of both its royal and its bus connections, after a century as a royal route and service to Deeside, the line closed in February 1966 to passengers and to goods in July of the same year.

Ballater station remains and today is used in part as a restaurant, shops and office. It still retains Queen Victoria's rooms. There have been plans to consider reopening a section of the branch as a tourist line, initially from Ballater to Cambus O' May and possibly eastward to Dinnet and Aboyne.

Above: The abandoned Aboyne station, looking east in February 1972. *A. Muckley*

Below: Dinnet station, looking towards Aberdeen in August 1965. *A. Muckley*

Above: The remains of Dinnet station and signalbox after closure and track lifting of one of the lines in May 1970. *A. Muckley*

Left: Dinnet station after the signalbox had been demolished, February 1972. *A. Muckley*

Above right: Cambus O' May, the next station down the line from Ballater, with a view looking from Ballater in August 1965. *A. Muckley*

Right: 'K2' No 61779 passing Cambus O' May in July 1953 with the River Dee in the foreground. *Ian Allan Library*

Below left: Timetable July 1955.

Table 40 · ABERDEEN and BALLATER

Miles		am	am	pm S	pm	pm		Miles		am	am	pm	pm	pm S
—	Aberdeen ... ... dep	8 11	1015	2 03	186	5		—	Ballater ... ... dep	7 20	1022	3 30		5 42
3¼	Cults	8 20	...	...	3 27	...		3¾	Cambus o'May Halt ...	...	...	3 37		
7½	Culter	8 30	...	...	3 34	...		6	Dinnet	7 31	1033	3 43		5 53
10½	Park	8 37	...	...	3 41	...		11	Aboyne	7 39	1041	3 51		6 1
14	Crathes	8 43	...	...	3 47	...		13½	Dess	7 45	...	3 57		
17	Banchory	8 49	1043	2 27	3 53	6 32		16½	Lumphanan	7 52	1052	4 4		6 12
21½	Glassel	9 0	...	4 36		42		19½	Torphins	7 58	11 04	4 12		6 18
23½	Torphins	9 7	11 1	2 43	4 13	6 48		21½	Glassel	8 3	...	4 17		
27	Lumphanan	9 15	11 9	2 51	4 21	6 56		26½	Banchory	8 12	1112	4 26		6 34
29¼	Dess	9 20	...	...	4 26	7 2		29½	Crathes	8 18	...	4 32		
32¼	Aboyne	9 26	1118	3 04	3 27			32¾	Park	...	...	4 38		
36¼	Dinnet	9 36	1128	3 104	42			35½	Culter	8 29	...	4 45		
39¼	Cambus o'May Halt ...	9 42	...	...				39½	Cults	8 35	...	4 51		
43¼	Ballater ... ... arr	9 49	1139	3 21	4 53	7 27		43¼	Aberdeen ... ... arr	8 43	1140	4 59	7 2	9 21

S Saturdays only

Above: Ballater station photographed in September 1967. The track was removed quite quickly from this end of the branch after closure. The substantial wooden station remains to this day and Victoria's waiting room is in use as an office. *Author*

Below: A general view of Ballater station on 14 September 1963. The coaching stock of the royal train was 'shedded' at Ballater whilst the Royal Family were in residence at Balmoral.

The coach sheds can be seen in the background of the photograph. *D. Simpson*

Right: A view of Ballater station, similar to that on the previous page, looking east in February 1972. The fact that the station was never intended as a terminus is clear. The use of the building on the left by a funeral director is in keeping with the general sombre scene. *A. Muckley.*

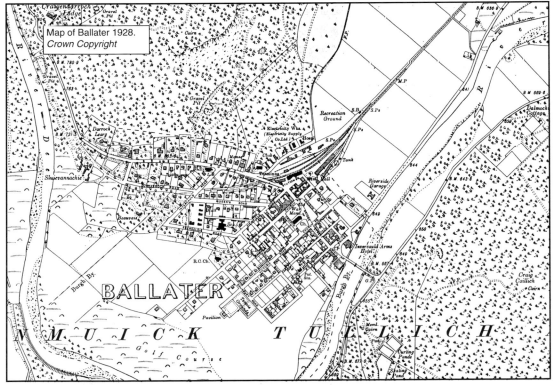

Map of Ballater 1928.
Crown Copyright

18 Speyside special

Queen Victoria was among those to appreciate the delights of the Spey Valley. The area is celebrated for its salmon fishing, but in particular is world renowned for its malt whisky and the many distilleries with their 0-4-0 'Whisky Pugs' brought prosperity to this part of Scotland. As a consequence, a surprising number of lines were built in this somewhat sparsely populated region. The area was also a battleground between the GNSR, with its aim to reach Inverness, and the HR's efforts, which in the end were largely effective in frustrating this.

The 33-mile Speyside Railway and later Great North of Scotland route from Boat of Garten to Craigellachie was not very heavily used nor very profitable from the beginning, although attempts to save money by using second hand rails during its construction were thwarted. Opened in August 1866, it ran from Boat of Garten via Grantown-on-Spey to the former junction at Craigellachie and later formed one of the most northerly sections of the LNER.

From Boat of Garten the line followed closely the broad and gently sloping valley of the River Spey in a

Below left: The station name board still *in situ* and awaiting the return of trains at Boat of Garten in February 1972. *A. Muckley*

Left: 4-4-0 No 49 *Gordon Highlander* and Jones Goods 4-6-0 No 103 soon after leaving Boat of Garten for the Speyside line with the RCTS Scottish Rail Tour special on 16 June 1962. *C. T. Gifford*

Above: Busy scene at Boat of Garten, looking towards Grantown-on-Spey in September 1978. *A. Muckley*

Right: Ex-CR 0-6-0 No 57591 at Boat of Garten on the 10.10 am from Craigellachie on 8 September 1955. *J. Emslie*

north-easterly direction and provided distant views of the Cairngorm and Monadhliath Mountains. It crossed the River Spey on two interesting and substantial, but completely different types of bridge. At Ballindalloch the line traversed the Spey on a lattice truss girder bridge built in 1863, with approach spans containing elegant cast iron railings. Contrasting with this bridge, but also built in 1863 by the Strathspey

Railway, was the Carron Bridge. This was constructed as a single cast iron arch with three bridge ribs. A road shared this bridge but, unlike Connel Bridge, where road and rail were separated by an iron kerb, at Carron the road was separated by a wall of slender cast iron plates.

The GNSR route along the Spey formed an inland link in a network of lines covering the area. At

Craigellachie the route joined the former GNSR Keith to Elgin line. This ran eastward to Keith, via Glen Fiddich and Dufftown, a station which from my diary records appeared to have been repainted just before passenger closure. The line also ran north from Craigellachie via Glen Rothes to Elgin.

The Speyside line closed to passengers in October 1965, followed by the route via Dufftown between Keith and Elgin in May 1968. Whisky traffic remained from Keith to Aberlour, the first station west of Craigellachie, until November 1971. The track is still in situ from Keith to Dufftown with plans for preservation, whilst the direct and former HR line between Keith and Elgin remains in use, forming part of the main Aberdeen to Inverness route.

On the Speyside line the fine bridges which were

Left: Grantown-on-Spey (East) station, looking towards Craigellachie in November 1970. *A. Muckley*

Below left: Ex-GNSR No 62262 heads a freight train approaching Grantown-on-Spey on the Speyside branch. *P. B. Whitehouse*

Right: Ex-CR 0-6-0 at Ballindalloch with a Craigellachie bound freight. *W. Anderson*

Below: BRCW Type 2 D5327 on a Craigellachie to Aviemore pick-up goods on 21 June 1967 between Dailuaine halt and Carron station. *J. Boyes*

Left: EE Type 1 D8032 on an Aviemore to Craigellachie pick up goods at Carron on 28 June 1966. *J. Boyes*

Below left: Ex-GNSR 4-4-0 No 62277 *Gordon Highlander* with the afternoon Boat of Garten train crosses the River Spey on the bridge at Carron on 19 August 1951. *W. Anderson*

Right: A rather sadder Carron station, looking towards Craigellachie in September 1977. *A. Muckley*

Below: Craigellachie, with a view of the Elgin line platform 2 with the sign to the Strathspey train on platform 3. The signs here, clearly designed to be helpful, look as cluttered as the variety of buildings that were provided for this station, *circa* 1950. *D. Lawrence*

well built to cope with the floodwaters of the Spey remain. Knockando station is employed as a whisky distiller's information centre. At the western and opposite end of the GNSR line from Craigellachie the branch met the Highland Railway (later the LMS) at Boat of Garten. From here the line ran on for a further 5 miles westward over HR tracks to Aviemore. It is this section of former HR line that has been preserved by the Strathspey Railway.

At Aviemore the Strathspey Railway Co has its own station, close to the restored engine shed, using buildings from Dalnaspidal, a footbridge from Longmorn

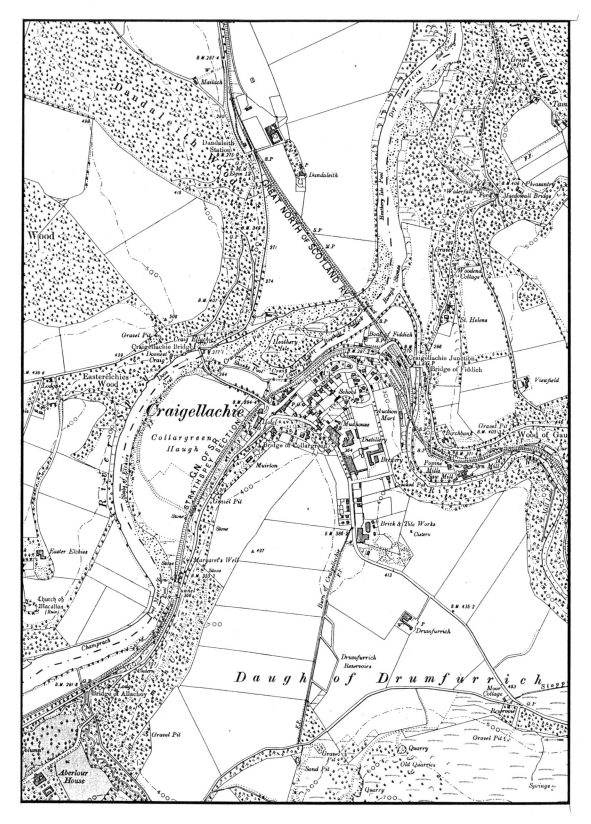

Above: Craigellachie Junction box with a DMU on the 11.40 Cairnie Junction to Elgin train via Craigellachie on 20 June 1967. *J. Boyes*

Right: Park Royal railbus No 79970 at Craigellachie with the 7.52 am Aviemore to Elgin service on 22 July 1959. *R. Furness*

Left: Map of Craigellachie Junction 1905. *Crown Copyright*

Above: A Park Royal railbus No 79970 leaves Boat of Garten with the midday Aviemore to Elgin service on 20 July 1959. *R. Furness*

Above right: Dufftown station on the 'Glen Line' in September 1967. It is interesting to note that the station which was due for closure had recently been partly repainted. *Author*

Above left: BRCW Type 2 D5327 with a Craigellachie to Aviemore pick-up goods at Craigellachie station on 21 June 1967. *J. Boyes*

Left: A similar view of Craigellachie station, but looking west with the Speyside branch diverging to the left, just three years later in May 1970. *A. Muckley*

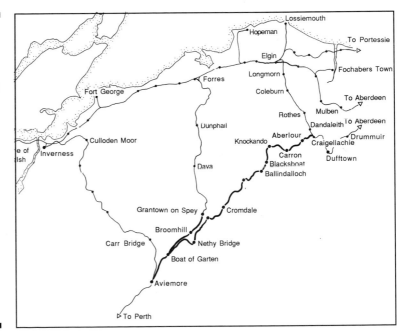

and a turntable from the Kyle of Lochalsh. The preserved line has an ex-LMS Black 5 No 5025, which in the past was regularly used as motive power on the Highland line, an ex-LMS 2-6-0 Ivatt locomotive and a number of industrial engines.

The preserved line runs north-eastward from Aviemore in the shadows of the Cairngorm Mountains (where nesting osprey have returned) towards Grantown-on-Spey, over what originally formed part of the HR's first trunk line from Perth to Inverness. Most of the HR line north of Boat of Garten, via Dunphail and over the 1,052ft Dava summit to Forres, whose nearby blasted heath may well have suggested the setting for Macbeth, closed in October 1965. This section of line, due to its height and exposure, had also been temporarily closed on other occasions by winter weather. Nevertheless, its final closure by BR was very many years after it had been replaced by the more direct HR line to Inverness via Carr Bridge.

19 Incident at Lentran

There were many wayside stations that served very small settlements. They were often built opportunistically to tap trade from settlements that happened to be located near the railway, or for operating reasons. They were a bonus to a line's revenue, but could turn into a liability when, as in some cases, more staff than passengers appeared to occupy little used wayside stations. As a consequence, many such stations closed prior to the Beeching cuts, including the one at Lentran on the southern shores of the Beauly Firth between Inverness and Dingwall, which closed in June 1960. Yet in an emergency and in the days before train radio contact such stations could still be useful. This was the case at Lentran where the station's passing loop had been retained, together with the signalbox and other buildings, all of which were in surprisingly good condition some seven years after closure of the station to regular passenger services. The diary records the breakdown of the Kyle train at this station:

19 JULY 1967; The train suddenly started to make more noise and masses of smoke billowed from it, covering the windows with a black oil. The train stopped and restarted, but the smoke and noise were worse. We just managed to limp into Lentran which caused quite a stir locally as trains no longer used or stopped at this station. Help was summoned from Inverness and in less than half an hour, after some nifty shunting, we were on our way with a replacement engine. We made up time and arrived at the Kyle only five minutes late.

Below: Preserved 'Black 5' No 5025 passes Lentran with a special train to the Kyle of Lochalsh for the Scottish Chamber Orchestra on 29 May 1982. *D. Cross*

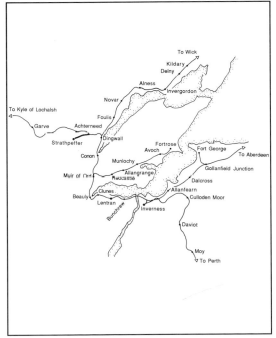

Top left: Although closed in June 1960, the station and signal cabin were in good condition in July 1967 when they were pressed into emergency use. *Author*

Top right: The arrival of the cavalry! A relief and distinctive-sounding Sulzer-engined Type 2 arrives from Inverness to replace its sister engine which had failed on the Kyle of Lochalsh train in July 1967. *Author*

Above: The passing loop came in useful; a neat piece of shunting replaced the broken down engine with a replacement. *Author*

20 The Strathpeffer Spa express

The Dingwall and Skye Railway, which became part of the Highland Railway and later the LMS, fairly uniquely for Scotland, met hostility from landowners in the Strathpeffer area and in particular from a Sir William Mackenzie. As a consequence, the main line to the Kyle of Lochalsh and Skye bypassed the sole centre of population west of Dingwall. The line, which remains open, deviates on a 1 in 50 gradient north of the spa town over a craggy mountain area south of Ben Wyvis near the Raven Rock, where a station at Achterneed was built rather inconveniently for Strathpeffer. Nevertheless, the route revealed an unparalleled area of the Scottish Highlands and provided fine views of Strathpeffer itself in the valley below.

Once Mackenzie was dead, antagonism to the railway ended and in June 1885 the Strathpeffer branch was opened from Fodderty Junction along a sheltered wooded valley to an attractive terminus. This had fan-like glazing bars in the platform canopy gables giving a bright and airy feel to the terminal which was located on the east side of the spa town some 5 miles west of Dingwall.

The Highland Railway made efforts to promote the spa town and at the height of the season through sleeping cars from the south were run on from Inverness to Strathpeffer, whilst the 'Strathpeffer Spa Express' ran non-stop from Aviemore, using the avoiding line at Inverness station, to Dingwall. Indeed, inclusive through tickets from other railway companies, such as the London and North Western, which included accommodation at the Highland Railway's Hotel, were available in the heyday of the spa town.

In spite of the attractive location and the fine facilities, including a golf course, the area suffered a very short season. Because of this the LMS were forced to

Below: After its closure to passengers in 1946 Strathpeffer station remained in an ever increasing derelict state, but in use as a coal merchant's office, as shown by this photograph taken in April 1966. *P. Foster*

Right: NRM Poster. The delights of Strathpeffer are outlined on this HR poster as 'The Fountain of Health' with the strongest sulphur waters in Europe.

Below: HR 0-4-4T No 55, *Strathpeffer.* The express was perhaps more a romantic title than a high speed service? *Ian Allan Library*

Bottom: By 1986 when this photograph was taken, the station had been restored and let to a number of small tourist-orientated companies. *Dr L. Nixon*

close the former HR's hotel in the town each winter. In addition, most trains to and from the town involved a change at Dingwall, which was inconvenient, and the line ultimately closed to passengers in February 1946 and to all traffic in 1951, with Achterneed once again becoming the nearest station for Strathpeffer until its closure in December 1964, although it reopened as a private halt the following year. The former HR's hotel which was sold off by BR in 1958 remains, together with the station buildings; indeed, the branch line was still shown as open on Bartholomew's World Atlas 1982 edition.

21 Kintyre casualty

Although never at any time part of the Scottish Region, in terms of interest the Campbeltown and Machrihanish Light Railway is well worth a mention. The 6-mile line crossed Kintyre from coast to coast near Aros Moss, and the canalised Machrihanish Water. This was a narrow and relatively flat area of the southern part of the peninsula that also contained coal reserves. A mineral line was opened in 1877 between Drumlemble Colliery and a coal discharging area at Campbeltown. In 1906 the line was relaid to a 2ft 3in gauge and extended from the Argyll Colliery to the Atlantic coast at Machrihanish and down a deep cutting into Hall Street at Campbeltown, and on to the quayside. Six intermediate halts were provided, and *Argyll* and *Atlantic* became natural choices for two of the engines that ran on the line.

An experimental passenger run was not particularly successful. The engine was derailed a number of times, but fortunately miners, who made up the majority of the passengers, were able to give assistance and on several occasions were required to manhandle the engine back on the rails. None the less, passenger services were initiated in August 1906 and a light railway order was ultimately acquired in 1908.

Right: Verandah view from one of the six Campbeltown and Machrihanish Railway carriages on 2 August 1930. Readers who saw the film *The Train* may recall a similar shot taken in France, only in that case the engine was heading for the coach at full speed! *H. C. Casserley*

Below: A passenger train waits in Hall Street on the waterfront at Campbeltown on 2 August 1930, the penultimate year of passenger services. *H. C. Casserley*

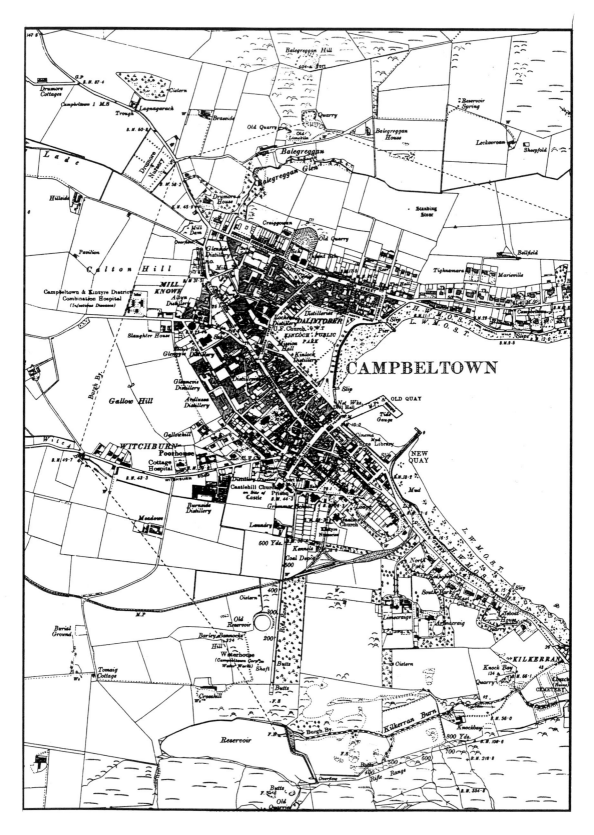

The line had a profitable summer tourist income, mainly as a result of tourists from the steamers that used Campbeltown, as the quay was situated within a few feet of the line's station in Hall Street. However, the short season of summer passenger traffic could not sustain the line all year. By the late 1920s coal traffic had very considerably declined and the finances of the railway had become a matter of some concern. The Argyll Colliery closed in 1929 and soon after both the railway and the colliery were acquired by the Maisel Oil Company who intended to produce oil from coal, but this proved uneconomic and the company folded.

Bus competition and the need for extensive repairs to the locomotives forced closure to passengers in September 1931, after a mere 25 years of such operation, and the line closed to all traffic in November 1932. The passenger rights were sold to the local bus operator. A liquidator was appointed in 1933 and the line was dismantled and the engines scrapped by 1934. Little trace of the railway remains today.

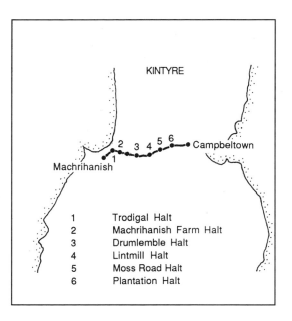

Below: 0-6-2T *Atlantic* at Campbeltown on 2 August 1930. The engine was scrapped in 1934. *H. C. Casserley*

Left: Map of Campbeltown 1924. *Crown Copyright*

Above: 0-6-2T *Argyll* at Campbeltown on 2 August 1930. The engine was scrapped three years later. *H. C. Casserley*

Below: 0-6-2T *Atlantic* with a train at the remote Machrihanish terminus on the Atlantic coast on 2 August 1930. *H. C. Casserley*

22 The Highlands by observation car

The breathtaking scenic potential of many Scottish lines was appreciated from the beginning and the NBR ran carriages with unusually large windows on the West Highland line. Observation cars ran over the Highland Railway from Perth to Aviemore, but it was Caledonian Railway's observation cars, manufactured by the Pullman Car Company, that provided some of the best views of the line. Each car was named after famous Scottish ladies such as Flora Macdonald. They were unique in that enormous rear bow windows were provided practically to floor level.

In the 1960s observation cars were still in use on the Highland lines. Principally they ran from Glasgow to Oban, from Fort William to Mallaig and from Inverness to the Kyle of Lochalsh. The services utilised observation cars discarded from other trains, such as the beaver-tailed observation cars from the LNER's East Coast main line dating from the corona-tion of King George VI. This type was used on the West Highland line, the LNER's two tone Cambridge and Garter blue having long since given way to BR's standard maroon. Equally historic, the former Southern Railway's 'Devon Belle' Pullman observation car was used on the Inverness to Kyle of Lochalsh line.

A single supplementary charge in 1967 for the West Highland Extension from Fort William to

Below: NRM Poster. A day out in the Highlands; absolute bliss!

Observation Coach Train at Lochy Viaduct near Fort William

THE WEST HIGHLAND LINE

 SEE BRITAIN BY TRAIN

Above and above right: A former 'Devon Belle' Pullman observation car at Kyle of Lochalsh on 19 July 1967. Refreshments were available from a small pantry at the rear of the car. Unlike the LNER beaver-tailed cars, the former SR car seating was fixed, but individual chairs were able to rotate. *Author*

Right: The observation car was turned on the old steam turntable at Kyle of Lochalsh as shown here on 9 July 1967. This has now been moved to the Speyside Railway at Aviemore. *Author*

Left: The interior of the beaver-tailed observation car on 26 July 1967 on the West Highland extension. Note the distinctive crown from the original use on the LNER's King George VI coronation trains. *Author*

Below: The interior of the observation car, also on 26 July 1967, coming off Glenfinnan viaduct. *Author*

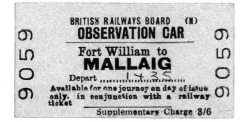

Mallaig was 3s 6d (17½p). Commentary was provided and a series of innocuous jokes replaced a dissertation on the route if the infamous Scotch Mist blotted out the view. The diary records some good fun on the West Highland observation car:

26 JULY 1967; The train arrived late at Fort William from Glasgow. This was the first train of the day, but does not arrive until midday. We set off for Mallaig, late, the conductor/ guide had a very strong Scottish accent and he sounded like a parrot. A small dog took a dislike to him and people chuckled when it pulled at his trousers. He went on endlessly about the new road to Mallaig, but did inform that steam trains on the line often got stuck, so they would have to divide the train which took half an hour. Only two diesels had been stuck. At Mallaig a man washes the windows each time.

These observation car services were eventually all withdrawn and for a number of years, apart from a brief revival in the 1980s, no observation cars ran in Scotland, with the exception of those in private ownership such as on the 'Royal Scotsman'. Then there was a change of mind. The present generation of observation car originates from a converted DMU and is used on the 82-mile Inverness to Kyle line, attached to a 'heritage' set of coaches.

Right: A former LNER beaver-tailed observation car at Mallaig on 26 July 1967, returning to the platform to have its windows washed, having been turned on the turntable. *Author*

Below: BRCW Type 2 No D5385 climbs away from Glenfinnan viaduct with a Mallaig to Fort William train on 15 July 1964 with an observation car on the rear. *P. Riley*

This book has concentrated on closed lines, yet in Scotland many lines of great interest remain; observation car or not, they are well worth seeing. Indeed, when admiring the views, romance and Burns come to mind, 'From scenes like these, old Scotia's grandeur springs!' See the lines that remain soon.

British Railways Board (H)
OBSERVATION CAR
Mallaig to
FORT WILLIAM
Depart.....
Available for one journey on day of issue only, in conjunction with a railway ticket. Supplementary Charge 3/6
1861   1861